so pretty!

FELT

so pretty! **FELT**

24 Stylish Projects to Make with Felt

Amy Palanjian

CHRONICLE BOOKS

SAN FRANCISCO

Library of Congress Cataloging-in-Publication Data:

Palanjian, Amy.
    So pretty! felt : 24 stylish projects to make with felt / by
Amy Palanjian ; illustrations by Julia Rothman.—1 [edition].
      p. cm.
    Includes index.
    ISBN 978-1-4521-0831-5
    1. Felt work. I. Rothman, Julia, illustrator. II. Title.
    TT849.5.P36 2013
    746'.0463—dc23
                              2012013903

Manufactured in China

Designed by Marina Sauri
Wardrobe styling by Jasmine Hamed
Prop styling by Christine Wolheim

Aleene's No-Sew Fabric Glue is a registered trademark of Duncan Enterprises. Coats & Clark Button & Craft Thread is a registered trademark of Coats & Clark Inc. DMC Embroidery Thread is a registered trademark of DMC Corp. Gingher's Knife-Edge Embroidery Scissors is a registered trademark of Fiskars Brands, Inc. Legos is a registered trademark of Lego Juris A/S Corp. Sakura Pigma Micron Pen is a registered trademark of Sakura Color Products Corp. Squeeze Die Cutter by QuicKutz is a registered trademark of Mark A. Hixon.

10 9 8 7 6 5 4 3 2 1

Chronicle Books LLC
680 Second Street
San Francisco, California 94107
www.chroniclebooks.com

CONTENTS

INTRO-DUCTION

uring one of my first magazine jobs years ago, I learned firsthand the intricacies and nuances of felt. The senior editor I was working with had me on the hunt for felt to form the base of a Christmas village, but not just any felt would do. She wanted the "good stuff"—the thick, supple 100-percent wool felt from Germany. It was extremely hard to find in the colors she wanted, but when the samples finally came to the office, I understood that she was entirely right: the wool felt was like nothing I had ever worked with. It wasn't thin and flimsy; it was thick and ever so slightly variegated in color. It had character, body, and a tactile quality that was irresistible. I was sold.

I've always remembered that experience. In fact, I still have a few leftover pieces from that work project tucked away in my fabric stash. They make me happy each time I come across them and are a good reminder of the importance of choosing quality in basic ingredients.

Since then, I've watched as more and more varieties of the "good stuff" have become available on the market. Felt, in its wide range of colors, has become a highly sought-after and attainable material for year-round craft projects. You don't have to felt your own pure wool in order to have a fantastic material to work with. Now you can simply purchase beautiful manufactured wool felt at high-quality craft shops! Not surprisingly, that influx has given rise to a new set of crafters who are turning simple sheets and rolls of felt into all manner of goods—like personal accessories, jewelry, clothing, housewares, and even items to use for a wedding.

The women featured in this collection of felting projects exemplify how crafting just one simple material can take so many different directions. I love how widely creative their projects are. I hope you will find inspiration in learning a bit about their lives and the context in which their crafts were born. From as far away as England and Poland and as close to home as right down the street, these felt crafters and their work represent the best of the best from around the world. From necklaces, earrings, and headbands, to garlands, mobiles, wreaths, pillows, bags, bouquets, corsages, pincushions, and more, there is plenty here to motivate you to make something yourself. And with basic crafting skills and little bit of your own ingenuity, you can turn any of these projects into your own unique felt creation.

So consider the stories and projects a jumping-off point for you in finding your own creative renewal. And don't forget to enjoy the planning of your project, the sourcing of the felt, and the actual steps of each woolen creation along the way.

—*Amy*

P.S. If you turn to the back of the book, you'll find templates included for many of the projects to make your crafting experience easier and more enjoyable.

TOOLS & TECH-NIQUES

To start crafting with felt and to make the projects in this book, you'll need relatively few supplies. Stock up on quality tools and notions, and they will serve you for years to come.

BEAD REAMER

A simple tool, available at jewelry and craft supply stores, a bead reamer can help you expand a too-small bead hole or punch a small, neat hole through felt.

CLASPS

Jewelry clasps can be used to hold necklaces and bracelets together. They come in many varieties—toggle, hook and eye, lobster claw, and magnetic, to name just a few—and are made of many materials. Look in the jewelry supplies aisle at your local craft store for the multitude of options.

CUTTING MAT

A cutting mat (with a rotary cutter and ruler) is the easiest way to make long, straight cuts in fabric and other materials. The cutting mat is made of self-healing material, so nicks and scratches disappear almost immediately.

DIE CUT MACHINE

This tool will cut specific shapes from paper or fabric using a stencil that's edged with a blade. The same effect can usually be achieved by hand with a template and slow and steady tracing and cutting.

DISAPPEARING FABRIC MARKER

Much like tailor's chalk, a disappearing fabric marker is used to mark fabric before cutting or altering. Most craft shops have a wide assortment of relatively inexpensive disappearing fabric markers, so try a few until you find your favorite.

EMBROIDERY NEEDLE

With a smaller eye than a darning needle but a larger eye than a sewing needle, this needle is the one to use with embroidery thread. Embroidery needles come in a range of sizes: pick the size you find most comfortable to work with.

EMBROIDERY THREAD

Often made with six strands twisted together, embroidery thread is used to embellish projects with colorful stitched patterns or to work very fine crochet. It is also known as embroidery floss and is available in many materials, including cotton, linen, metallic, and rayon.

FELTING NEEDLE

A felting needle allows you to tack one piece of felt or wool to another using repetitive piercings.

FUSIBLE INTERFACING

Usually sold in sheets or rolls, this webbed material is often made from polyester or nylon. It has an iron-on capacity, and is used to add sturdiness and durability to regular fabric.

GLUE GUN AND GLUE STICKS

The hot glue gun is still a staple crafting tool, and if you haven't used one since you were a kid, have no fear—they are virtually the same. Keep in mind that a little bit of glue goes a long way, so you can usually get by with a small glue gun model and light pressure on the trigger. Remember to keep extra glue sticks on hand.

IRON AND IRONING BOARD

Having an iron and ironing board set up and ready to use while you work can save you time when you need to iron out creases in fabric or felt. And taking the time to iron a seam as directed before sewing it can make the assembly process infinitely easier.

JUMP RING

Jump rings are used in jewelry making to connect one element with another. The jump ring is typically made out of material that is similar to that of the necklace or bracelet.

PINKING SHEARS

Fitted with a sawtooth blade, these scissors cut a zigzag edge that prevents fabric from unraveling or fraying. They can give an instant finish to the edges of felt.

PINS

A collection of straight pins is a must for sewing and felt projects. You'll find that thinner pins will be gentler on your fabric, so buy different kinds at the craft store to find the ones you like best. You will also occasionally need safety pins of different sizes; large ones, for instance, can be used to thread elastic or twill tape through a fabric drawstring casing.

PLIERS

A small pair of pliers (found in the jewelry supply section of most craft stores) can come in very handy. Pick up the type specified in each project (such as crimping pliers, which are specifically used to flatten crimp beads, or round-nose pliers, which are useful for making small loops in wire) for the best outcome possible. Needle-nose pliers are a good all-purpose option.

ROTARY CUTTER

Similar to a pizza cutter, a rotary cutter has a circular blade and a handle. When used with a cutting mat and ruler, it is the easiest way to make accurate, straight cuts on large pieces of fabric.

RULER

You can use a regular foot-long ruler for your craft projects. But I suggest picking up a plastic quilting ruler, which is clear and has an inch-by-inch grid so that you can see through it and can easily measure most materials.

SCISSORS

You will need a large pair of fabric scissors to cut large pieces of felt or fabric. You will also need small scissors for most projects in the book, which will fit into a portable sewing kit. Gingher's 4- or 5-in/10- to 12-cm Knife-Edge Embroidery Scissors come with a protective cover for safe storage and are sharp enough to prevent your yarn or thread from fraying when you snip (available at gingher.com). A pair of blunt-edge baby scissors (available at most drugstores) is also a safe option for crafters with kids (or pets) around.

SEWING MACHINE

A few projects suggest using a sewing machine, which will make quick work of sewing seams. But all the projects can be completed with hand-stitches.

SEWING NEEDLES

You'll want to have a good supply of basic sewing needles on hand. They are thinner and have smaller eyes than embroidery needles. Needles that are specifically for hand-quilting are a good option for more precise stitching because they tend to be even thinner and available in many lengths (it's best to purchase a few and find your favorite).

SEWING THREAD

Some inexpensive sewing thread is of poor quality and breaks easily, so look for good-quality cotton thread such as hand-quilting thread by Gütermann or cotton-covered polyester Button & Craft thread by Coats & Clark. Both are strong, durable options.

TAILOR'S CHALK

Used to mark fabric for cutting (or altering), this type of chalk easily rubs off of fabric.

TRANSFER PAPER

Have you ever used carbon paper? Transfer paper is similar, but one side is lined with chalk. When you place this paper over your fabric and trace the outline of a shape, chalk lines will transfer onto the fabric.

TWILL TAPE

Often used as backing for buttons to reinforce their sewn stitches, or for drawstrings, twill tape comes in many types, widths, and colors and is sold at fabric shops.

WIRE CUTTERS

Wire cutters are a helpful tool for cutting quickly and efficiently through wire. If a project calls for wire cutters, try to use them—the toughness of wire can damage scissors, especially sewing scissors meant for fabric.

FELT FACTS

HOW TO SELECT FELT

Wool felt is a naturally durable fabric. It's made when woolen fibers are first matted and tangled together through abrasion (rather than woven like most other fabrics), and then the fibers are exposed to heat, which shrinks the material and further enmeshes the fibers. The combination of abrasion and heat makes the wool fabric dense and strong.

Felt comes in 100-percent wool, combined wool and other substances, as well as synthetic varieties, and choice is a matter of personal preference. If you want the best experience, I suggest using pure wool felt, as specified throughout this book, because it will probably handle better and hold up longer. Manufactured sheets of this type of felt are widely sold in varying sizes and thicknesses, so choose the one that's best for the project you are doing.

HOW TO CARE FOR FELT

Follow these simple steps to treat your felt right and ensure that your projects turn out as beautifully as possible.

Wash Felt by Hand

The safest way to wash a felt item is to wash it by hand. Let the item soak in cool water and a tiny bit of mild detergent. Using your fingers, gently massage out any stains. Carefully squeeze the water out and allow the item to dry flat on a towel.

Avoid Hot Water

Using hot water will cause the felt item to shrink or become distorted.

Treat Stains Right Away

Felt naturally repels moisture, so it is inherently durable. But in the event that you do get a stain on your felt item, treat it promptly and gently before the stain has a chance to be absorbed and to set.

Avoid the Washing Machine

You can wash a felt item with cold water in the washing machine on the gentle cycle, but you run the risk of distorting the item. Use caution, treat the felt item like you would your most delicate pieces of clothing, and stick to hand washing when necessary.

HOW TO FELT

You can easily make your own wool felt from vintage or out-of-use sweaters. Here's how:

1. Use sweaters of 100-percent wool, or ones that are made mostly of wool, to start with. Each combination of materials (even wool and acrylic) will work slightly differently, so consider picking up sweaters of different combinations at a local thrift store and experimenting.

2. Wash one to three sweaters with one or two pairs of old, well-washed jeans—which just help to agitate the wool fibers—in a top-loading washing machine on the hot water cycle with high agitation.

3. Place the washed sweaters in the dryer and dry on high heat.

4. Smooth the sweaters flat and cut off any trim, edges, and the sleeves. You will have large pieces of felt to use. Save the sleeves for smaller projects.

In the projects, we use a few embroidery stitches. Here's how to make these basic stitches:

BACKSTITCH

To make a backstitch, which can be stronger than a simple running stitch, start with your thread on the stitch line. Then, take a small backward stitch. Bring the needle through again a bit in front of the first stitch and take another stitch, inserting the needle at the point where it first came through.

BLANKET STITCH

This stitch is commonly used as a decorative edge stitch, and is also used to appliqué a layer of fabric onto another layer of fabric. You can create a variety of looks with this stitch by varying the length and depth of the stitch, and by using different thicknesses of thread. Starting with the thread at the edge of the fabric, bring the threaded needle one stitch length to the left, and put it through the fabric, hooking the thread behind the needle tip. Pull the needle up to close the stitch so the thread is lying on the right edge of your work. Bring the needle over one stitch length again and repeat until you have the desired number of stitches.

CROSS-STITCH

This stitch, which is made by sewing one stitch over another in an X shape, is very easy to master. When working cross-stitch freehand (as is called for in this book), try to make your stitches a consistent length. But remember that part of the joy of freehand stitching is in the imperfection.

DETACHED CHAIN OR LAZY DAISY STITCH

This stitch, which can go by either name, is usually done in a circle to make a floral motif. Bring the needle up through your fabric and hold the thread with your left thumb. Insert the needle back into where it first came through the fabric. Place the needle through the fabric, bringing the tip of the needle out a short distance away. Wrap the thread under the needle tip and pull the needle through the fabric. Use a small stitch to fasten the loop you just made.

FRENCH KNOT

A French knot, which sounds as fancy as it looks, is made by wrapping floss (or thread or yarn) around your needle as you stitch. The knots that result are pearl-like and can be used to add simple dimension to your work. To make the stitch, place your needle from the wrong side of the fabric through to the right side. Wrap the thread around the needle twice and reinsert the needle into the fabric very close to where it originally came through. Be sure to pull the thread snugly before pulling the needle all the way through, so that the knot is on the surface of the fabric.

RUNNING STITCH

A basic straight stitch, a running stitch can be used to baste fabric or as a decorative embroidery stitch. Insert your needle several times in even intervals along the line where you want to sew. Pull the needle and thread through. You can also do one stitch at a time if that works best for you for the project at hand.

WHIPSTITCH

Whipstitching two pieces of felt together is one of the simplest joining techniques. Place two felt pieces together and, starting on the right side, take your needle threaded with embroidery floss and go from the inside of the bottom layer through to the outside. The goal is to have the knot at the end of your floss become sandwiched between the two layers of felt. Put the needle through the top layer above where the floss comes out of the bottom layer. Insert the needle through the original hole in the bottom layer. Pull it through both layers. Insert the needle through the existing hole in the top layer at a slight angle so the tip comes out of the bottom layer about $\frac{1}{8}$ in/3 mm to the left of the first stitch. Pull the needle through both layers. Repeat as needed.

PROJECTS

YOKO VEGA

LOS ANGELES, CALIFORNIA, AND JAPAN

It's almost guaranteed that you'll fall for the work of someone who describes her creations as "light and colorful pieces that make you want to eat candy"! Yoko Vega, who was born in Japan and frequently returns there from her home base in Los Angeles, makes pieces that are intricate and precise. "My grandmother taught me how to sew and make a skirt in sixth grade," she says. "I was the smallest kid in my school, but I wanted to wear adult clothes, so I asked her to teach me how to make them." Working out of her home, on items including accessories and children's clothing, she prefers to work when the weather is nice, imbuing her pieces with a cheerful nuance. In an effort to continually keep her work fresh and new, she explains, "I try not to get stuck making the same thing over and over, even if a particular item keeps selling." Yoko finds particular inspiration in vintage fabrics, flea markets, and antique furniture.

"In a sense, since felt is very durable and doesn't fray, it allows me to be very precise with my designs."

Perky, with a polka dot look, this bib necklace is surprisingly straightforward to make. Wear it with anything from a plain white tank to a dressier ensemble, and be ready to have your lovely self become the center of attention.

MATERIALS

1½-by-1½-in/4-by-4-cm piece of 1-mm-thick wool felt, navy blue

1½-by-1½-in/4-by-4-cm piece of 1-mm-thick wool felt, lilac

1½-by-1½-in/4-by-4-cm piece of 1-mm-thick wool felt, gray

1½-by-1½-in/4-by-4-cm piece of 1-mm-thick wool felt, ivory

6-by-4-in/15-by-10-cm piece of 2- to 2.5-mm-thick wool felt, ivory, for a base

Fabric glue (such as Aleene's No-Sew Fabric Glue)

Spool of sewing thread, off-white or ivory

Seven 3-mm-diameter ivory pearls

Silver-colored 1.8-mm chain, 14 in/35.5 cm long

Silver-colored clasp with attachment

2 silver-colored 4-mm jump rings

TOOLS

½-in/12-mm Circle Template

Pencil

Scissors

Flat, heavy weight (such as a ream of paper or an iron)

Beading needle (or any thin needle small enough to go through the beads)

Wire cutters

Needle-nose pliers

To make your circles precise, use a die cut tool with an appropriate-size die or the Circle template.

The thickness of felt is specified in this project to maintain the delicacy of the necklace. It will work with thicker felt, though the final result may be slightly more chunky looking and feeling.

1 With the ½-in/12-mm Circle Template, trace and cut out 4 circles each from the 1-mm-thick felt in navy blue, lilac, gray, and ivory, for a total of 16 circles.

2 Apply the fabric glue to one side of 1 of the 16 circles, and attach it to the 6-by-4-in/15-by-10-cm base piece of felt (see photo, page 28); repeat this process for the remaining 15 circles. It's especially important to put the glue on the circles, not on the felt base, and to cover as much of the surface of each felt circle as you can with glue. Carefully wipe off any glue that seeps out from behind the circles.

3 After arranging all of the circles on the base, place the weight on top of the glued felt pieces. If the surface of the weight is dirty, use a piece of paper between the felt and the weight. Let sit for 2 hours.

4 Once the glue has set, trim away the extra base felt to leave only the arranged circles.

5 With the needle and thread, sew the 7 pearls onto the spaces in the felt base between the circles. There is no specific placement of the pearls; just place them so they look pleasing to you. Knot the thread at each pearl to secure.

6 Cut the chain in half with wire cutters and sew each end of the chain to the outermost felt dot on each end of the piece. Stitch around four times to securely attach the chain, and then knot the thread to secure.

7 At the loose ends on the chain, attach the clasp with the jump rings, using the needle-nose pliers.

* Make the circles smaller or larger to play with the scale of the necklace.

* Use thin leather cord in place of the chain, or use a chain of a different material if that suits your fancy.

* Substitute the pearls for sparkly beads, or skip them altogether.

They say that each snowflake is unique; and the same is true for this delightfully whimsical necklace. Plus, any project that involves making ruffles is a surefire hit.

MATERIALS

12-by-4-in/30.5-by-10-cm piece of 1- to 1.5-mm-thick wool felt, in any color

Sewing thread to match the felt

Two 8-mm gold-colored jump rings

Gold-colored chain 13 in/33 cm long, in a link size of your choosing

Four 4-mm gold-colored jump rings

Gold-colored clasp

Pen

Clear gridded ruler

One 8½-by-11-in/21.5-by-28-cm sheet of paper

Rotary cutter

Cutting mat

TOOLS

Pins

Scissors

Sewing needle

Needle-nose pliers

Wire cutters

Try to use felt in the thickness called for since using thicker felt will make it more difficult to make delicate loops for the snowflakes.

1 With the pen and ruler, draw a straight line across the paper. Draw another line parallel with the first line ⅞ in/2.25 cm away. Then draw a third line parallel with the first line 1⅛ in/ 3 cm away.

2 Using the rotary cutter, ruler, and cutting mat, cut 9 strips of the felt each measuring 12 by ⅜ in/30.5 by 1 cm. To make each snowflake, you will need 3 strips.

3 The lines drawn on paper in Step 1 will be your guides to the folding pattern of the felt strips. Lay 1 felt strip on the paper with a short end lined up with the first line. Then fold the strip at the third line (1⅛ in/3 cm) and back to the first line, accordion style. Then fold the strip at the second line (⅞ in/2.25 cm) and back to the first line. Continue in this fashion, alternating the length of each fold, until the entire strip is folded. Secure this folded strip by sticking a pin through all the layers. Repeat with the other 3 strips.

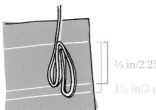

⅞ in/2.25 cm

1⅛ in/3 cm

4 Stack the 3 strips together, and align all the strips along the evenly folded edges. Count the number of folds on the uneven edge: you want 12 folds on that edge, but you will probably have a few more. Cut off any excess folds at the evenly folded edge. Then stick a pin through all the layers of the strips, and repeat on the opposite side. Cut any excess length of felt from the felt strips along the even side.

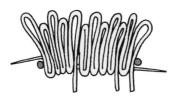

5 Thread the sewing needle and tie both ends of the thread together in a knot. With the needle and thread, sew the even side folds together by running the needle through all the layers once. When the layers are securely sewn together, remove the pins.

6 Fan out the uneven side of the strips and sew one end to the other, so the strips now form a circle. Tie a knot to secure the thread, and cut the thread.

7 Repeat Steps 3 through 6 with the remaining strips, so you end up with 3 circular felt snowflakes.

8 Arrange the 3 snowflakes as pictured, so a few of the folds or points touch or overlap slightly. Sew together the points that are touching with a small backstitch. Make sure that all 3 snowflakes are securely sewn together.

9 Using the needle-nose pliers, slightly open up the ends of the 8-mm gold-colored jump rings. With the snowflakes lying flat, locate the topmost fold on each of the outer snowflakes. Loop an 8-mm jump ring through each of these folds and close the jump ring with the pliers.

10 Cut the chain in half with wire cutters and attach one piece of the chain to each of the 8-mm jump rings, using a 4-mm gold-colored jump ring to join each side. At the other ends on the chain, attach the clasp with the remaining two 4-mm jump rings.

VARIATIONS

∗ Simplify and make a necklace with just one snowflake.

∗ Make your snowflakes out of three different colors of felt.

∗ Use a thin leather cord or a chain in a different material if desired.

STEPHANIE MONROE

BROOKLYN, NEW YORK

A few years ago, Stephanie, a graphic designer by trade, started working with felt when she received a project commission from a local earth-friendly toy store. From the project, Stephanie developed a love for felt. "What I like most about working with one-hundred-percent wool felt is the texture and thickness of it," she says. "It's the best material for hand embroidery—it's like the material was made especially for it—and since it has no raw edges, finishing a piece is very simple. I also love the fact that it comes from a living creature, which is just one more way for me to stay connected to Earth." Connections to life around her provide inspiration for her work, she says: "If I'm not designing new pieces for my store, I'm photographing turtles swimming in the pond, creating polymer clay cupcakes with my daughter, or designing new packaging for some product I imagine creating some day."

"As an artist, my creative lifestyle is a part of my everyday life. I live it, breathe it, and see it in everything I do."

FIND STEPHANIE

Stephaniemonroe.etsy.com   Thehoneypietree.typepad.com   Twitter.com/thehoneypietree
Facebook.com/thehoneypietree

Dress up a tray of cupcakes or even a cake with these cheerful easy-to-make toppers. They are a simple way to set the mood of a party without saying a word.

MATERIALS

Six 2-by-4-in/5-by-10-cm pieces of wool felt, in assorted colors (such as bright red, bubblegum pink, orange, peach, turquoise, and light blue)

Skein of cotton embroidery thread, cream or natural

6 round wooden toothpicks

TOOLS

Cupcake Toppers Template

Disappearing fabric marker

Scissors

Transfer paper in a light color or fine-tipped black pen (0.3 mm thick, such as Pigma Micron)

Pencil (if using transfer paper)

Embroidery needle

Glue gun and glue sticks

1 Using the diamond in the Cupcake Toppers Template and a disappearing fabric marker, trace a diamond onto 1 piece of felt. Cut out the diamond. Repeat for the remaining 5 pieces of felt. Each diamond will eventually be folded in half to make the triangular flag. Each letter should be sewn on the right side of the open flag so that it is visible when glued together.

2 Transfer the C-H-E-E-R-S letters from the template to the diamonds. Sandwich a piece of transfer paper, chalk side down, between a felt diamond and a printed letter that will be used (either from the Cupcake Toppers Template or you can look for fonts online). Using the pencil, trace over the letter with medium to heavy pressure so that the letter is easily visible. Repeat for the remaining 5 letters. Remember to trace each letter facing the same direction on each diamond piece, about ¼ in/ 6 mm to the right of where you will fold the diamond in half. No time for tracing? Just draw the letters on the felt without a template using the fine-tipped black pen.

3 Cut a piece of embroidery thread from the skein that is about 24 in/60 cm long. Thread your embroidery needle using 3 strands of the embroidery thread. Pull the thread through the needle so that both ends match up and secure the ends in a knot.

4 Using a backstitch, embroider a letter onto each diamond. After stitching a letter, be sure to secure the thread with a knot on the wrong side so the ends are not visible.

5 Turn the diamonds over so that the wrong side is facing up. (You will want the letters to be backward with the top of the letters pointing away from you. Using the hot glue gun, place a small amount of glue along the center of 1 diamond. Position the top ¼ to ⅓ of a toothpick onto the glue. After the toothpick is secured in place, use the glue gun to trace along one half of the diamond with a small amount of glue.

6 Pick up the topper by the toothpick and fold the diamond in half, sandwiching the toothpick between the two sides. Move as quickly as possible, because the hot glue cools quickly. The end result will be a triangular flag pointing to the right. Repeat this step for the remaining 5 toppers until you spell C-H-E-E-R-S.

7 Find the yummiest, most delectable cupcakes or cake and stick in the toppers, giving them a happy home.

VARIATIONS

* Spell out the guest of honor's name for a personalized touch at a celebration.

* Simplify and make just one or two toppers with the age of the birthday girl or boy.

* Embellish the toppers with beads, sequins, or rickrack for a more festive touch.

This sweet, petite bag is perfect for holding jewelry and little odds and ends. It also makes a darling gift bag for a special present, or is a cute gift all on its own. Make one for yourself and for all your friends!

MATERIALS

9-by-11-in/23-by-28-cm sheet of wool felt, light blue

9-by-11-in/23-by-28-cm sheet of wool felt, tangerine

1-by-1-in/2.5-by-2.5-cm square scrap of wool felt, hot pink

Cotton embroidery thread, hot pink, light orange, light blue, and yellow

Cotton sewing thread, cream

¾ yd/67 cm cotton twill tape ½ in/ 12 mm, natural

TOOLS

Birdie Bag Template

Disappearing fabric marker or a fine-tipped black pen (like a 0.5 mm Pigma Micron)

Scissors

Pins

Embroidery needle

Sewing machine

Safety pin

1 Using the rectangle in the Birdie Bag Template and a disappearing fabric marker (or a fine-tipped black pen), trace and cut 2 rectangles, 1 for the front and 1 for the back of the pouch, out of the light blue felt.

2 Using the bird and leaf in the same template, trace and cut out 2 birds and 1 tiny leaf of the tangerine wool felt. Then, trace and cut out 1 tiny leaf of the scrap of hot pink felt.

3 Arrange the birds on 1 of the felt rectangles, as shown or to your liking, and pin them to the felt. Using the disappearing fabric marker, mark 2 dots for the eyes and 3 dots for the "berry" French knots.

4 Using the light orange embroidery thread, blanket stitch the birds onto the light blue felt rectangle, which will be the front of the finished bag. Embroider both of the leaves below the birds with a backstitch, using the light orange embroidery thread on the hot pink leaf and the hot pink embroidery thread on the tangerine leaf. Then, using French knots, embroider 1 eye for each bird (using light blue embroidery thread), 2 berries (using yellow thread), and 1 berry (using hot pink) above the leaves.

5 Fold the top edge of the embroidered front rectangle down 1 in/2.5 cm with right sides together and pin. Using the sewing machine and cream-colored sewing thread, stitch a straight line along the bottom raw edge, making sure to backstitch at both ends. Repeat this step with the other rectangle for the back of the bag. You should have a drawstring casing about 1 in/2.5 cm wide at the top of both the front and back pieces of the bag.

6 Since the raw edges won't fray, you can sew the bag with right sides facing out. Align all edges, and pin both bag pieces together with right sides facing out. Starting at the casing stitching with a ⅛-in/3-mm seam allowance, sew the bag together, pivoting at each bottom corner and stopping at the casing stitching on the opposite side of the bag. Be sure to backstitch at the beginning and the end of this seam.

7 Cut your piece of twill tape in half. Take one of the twill tape pieces and attach the safety pin to one of the short raw edges. Starting at one side of the bag, feed the safety pin edge of the twill tape through the casing opening, and continue feeding the twill tape through the casing on the other side, so both short raw edges of the twill tape exit on the same side of the bag. Repeat with the other piece of twill tape and feed it through the casing on the opposite side of the bag. Tie the twill tape raw edges into a knot to join the ends, or flip the ends of the twill tape so the wrong sides are facing out, then sew a reinforcing zigzag stitch along the raw edges.

8 Close the bag by gently pulling the drawstrings in the opposite directions.

VARIATIONS

✳ Change the size of the bag so that it will hold an iPhone, iPad, or e-reader.

✳ Use a seasonal color palette to turn little bags into holiday gift bags.

✳ Adorn with your own creative embellishments in place of the birds.

FAITH LEX

EASTON, PENNSYLVANIA

"**W**hen I was ten, I did a one-year stint with the Girl Scouts where I was introduced to counted cross-stitch—that was when my love for hand-stitching began," explains Faith. "So, a few years ago when I couldn't find hair clips that I liked for my daughter, it made sense to make them myself." Faith had learned the basics of sewing, as well as knitting and crochet, from both her grandmother and mother, and she plans to pass on her own skills to her three children. "It's wonderful when women pass down their love of sewing, baking, and design to their children: like a family story that gets passed down through generations, except this story is told with your hands." Faith's daily life infuses her work—creative elements have a classic foundation combined with a bit of whimsy. Inspired by her quiet country surroundings—the small details in natural elements such as a leaf, a rock, or a sunrise—she enjoys working with felt because she says it's as if the material itself challenges her to be creative.

"I think it's important to remember that creativity can be an outlet for unwinding, and while it can't be a priority all of the time, it should be a priority some of the time."

FIND FAITH

Ordinarymommydesign.com   Ordinarymommy.etsy.com   Twitter.com/ordinarymommy

These delicate, dressed-up bobby pins are the perfect solution to a bad hair day. Use them to pin down too-long bangs or to accessorize a simple ponytail.

MATERIALS

9-by-5-in/23-by-12-cm piece of wool felt, in a color of your choosing

Skein of embroidery thread, in a color to match your felt

2 bobby pins

TOOLS

1-in/2.5-cm Circle Template

Scissors

Sewing needle

1 With the 1-in/2.5-cm Circle Template, trace and cut 14 circles from the felt. Separate the circles into 2 groups of 7, 1 stack for each rosette.

2 Working with 1 group, set aside 2 circles, 1 for the base and 1 for the back. The remaining 5 circles will be the petals.

3 Cut a 20-in/50-cm length of embroidery thread off of the skein. Separate it into 2 sections of 3 strands each; 1 section should be enough floss for 1 rosette. Thread the needle and knot the long end of the thread.

4 Take one of the petal circles and fold it in half twice so it is a quarter of its original size. Place it on top of the base circle, putting the point of the petal in the center of the base and keeping the wider part of the circle toward the outside. Bring the needle up through the back of the base circle and point of the folded petal, then bring the needle back down through the petal and base to tack in place.

5 Repeat Step 4 to tack down 3 more folded petals until the base is covered with 4 petals.

6 Bring the needle up through the center of the base again, being careful not to catch any of the existing petals. Fold the remaining petal in quarters and thread onto the needle. Pass the needle back through the center of the base, making sure not to catch any of the other petals. Pull the thread tight and tie a knot at the back of the base. Cut the thread.

7 Stitch the closed end of the bobby pin tightly onto the center of the backing circle with the needle and thread, passing the needle through it several times to make it secure.

8 Sew the backing circle onto the rosette with a running stitch around the perimeter of the rosette, 1/8 in/3 mm from the edge. Hold the petals back as you sew the backing on to avoid stitching them down. Tack down the bobby pin as you go to keep the rosette flat against the head when worn. When the backing is completely sewn to the rosette, tie a knot in the thread. Then pass the needle back through the layers of the rosette, coming out on the opposite side and cut the thread. Fluff up your rosette.

9 Repeat Steps 2–8 to make another Rosette Hairpin.

VARIATIONS

∗ Make more than two rosettes and use them to accessorize an up-do for a fancy occasion.

∗ Turn the rosettes into a wrist corsage by sewing two onto a length of ribbon and tying it on to wear.

∗ Make a cluster of rosettes and sew them onto the lapel of a sweater that needs a little adornment.

Proms, weddings, and special-occasion brunches aren't the only times when a corsage is called for. Simply add this pretty pin to a cardigan, plain dress, or basic white T-shirt and consider yourself best in show.

MATERIALS

8-by-7-in/20-by-17-cm piece of wool felt for the flower, in a color of your choosing

2¼-by-2-in/5.5-by-5-cm piece of wool felt for the leaf, green

Skein of embroidery thread to match the flower color

Bar pin

TOOLS

2-in/5-cm Circle Template

Pencil

Scissors

1¼-in/3.25-cm Circle Template

Carnation Corsage Template

Sewing needle

HELPFUL HINT

When placing the leaf, be sure to keep its relationship to the bar pin in mind. This will determine where the leaf sits when the flower is pinned.

1 With the 2-in/5-cm Circle Template, trace and cut out 2 circles from the felt for the flower. These will be the base and backing for the flower.

2 With the 1¼-in/3.25-cm Circle Template, trace and cut out 10 circles from the same piece of felt used in Step 1. These will be the petals.

3 With the Carnation Corsage Template, trace and cut out a leaf shape from the green felt.

4 Cut a 28-in/70-cm length of embroidery thread off of the skein. Separate it into 2 sections of 3 strands each; both of these sections should be enough for the entire project. Thread the needle and knot the long end of the thread.

5 Fold a petal circle in half and place it on the large base circle, putting the rounded edge of the petal along the outside of the base. Bring the needle up through the back of the base circle and through both layers of the petal about ¼ in/6 mm from one end of the fold. Tack the petal to the base using two stitches to form an X.

6 Take another petal circle, fold it in half, and place it on top of the previous petal, overlapping about a third of the existing petal. Tack it in place by coming through the base, the underlying petal, and just 1 layer of the top petal. By tacking down just 1 layer of the top petal, the petal will stay in place and remain fluffed.

7 Repeat Step 6 for petals 3–7. Slip the last petal underneath the first petal in the row. Then the first petal will need to be tacked down like the rest.

8 There should be 3 petal circles left for the center of the flower. Take 1 of them and fold it in half twice so it is a quarter of the original size. Bring the needle up through the back of the base and the point of the folded petal, then bring the needle back down through the petal and base to tack in place.

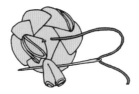

9 Moving a third of the way around the middle of the flower each time, repeat Step 8 with the remaining 2 petals.

10 Sew the bar pin to the large backing circle. To neaten up the back, cut a scrap of felt into a rectangle and, using a backstitch, sew a patch over the base of the bar pin.

11 Sew a backstitch around the perimeter of the leaf, about ⅛ in/3 mm from the edge. Place the leaf between the backing and the flower. Allow the leaf to stick out as far as you like. Holding the leaf in place, sew the backing of the corsage onto the flower with a running stitch about ⅛ in/3 mm from the edge. Hold the petals back as you sew to avoid stitching them down. When the backing is completely sewn to the flower, tie a knot in the thread. Then pass the needle back through the layers of the corsage, come out on the opposite side, and cut the thread.

VARIATIONS

* Add stitching to the edging of the leaf for added interest.

* To make your corsage more formal (and simpler), skip the leaf.

* To make a bigger flower, simply increase the size of both circle templates by ¼ in/6 mm.

LINDY CLINE

CHICAGO, ILLINOIS

Lindy was raised in a household filled with creativity. "My dad and brother are artists and my mom and I have always shared a love of projects. She was actually my first-grade teacher, so she taught me all the important stuff, how to read and write—and the fun stuff like sewing and baking," she says. And even when she was a kid, Lindy found felt mysterious. "I've always been intrigued by the feel and aesthetic that felted goods have. Felt can look so delicate or whimsical, but still be such a strong material." When it comes to her grown-up felt creations, she is inspired by many vintage treasures culled from her grandmother's home. "I prefer a clean, modern style and I love midcentury modern and vintage housewares," says Lindy. As a city dweller, she's space-challenged, but having the hustle and bustle of the city just outside the door fuels her creative energy. When she's not creating with felt, Lindy might be gardening or eating tacos—which would be lovely served on a table adorned with some of her projects.

"I love that my work uses traditional processes like knitting and sewing to create something modern and new."

FIND LINDY
Plytextiles.etsy.com

This graphic topper brings a sophisticated yet handmade touch to any table. Try it in the center of a dining table with a vase of flowers or candles, on a dresser, or on a side table.

MATERIALS

3 recycled wool sweaters in 3 different colors or three 9-by-12-in/23-by-30.5-cm sheets of wool felt in different colors

Sewing thread in coordinating colors

$5/8$ yd/60 cm fusible web, 17 in/43 cm wide

$1/3$ yd/30.5 cm of wool-blend felt, 36 in/1 m wide, for backing

TOOLS

Graphic Table Runner Template

Ruler

Scissors

Rotary cutter

Cutting mat

Sewing machine

Pencil

Iron and ironing board

1 Decide on colors to use for the table runner. If using old sweaters, felt them (see page 20 to learn how easy it is).

2 After the sweaters are felted and dry, cut them apart: Cut the sleeves off first in a straight line, then cut the side and shoulder seams of the body, then the seam of the sleeve. Depending on how much the sweaters shrank, you should have 4 good-size pieces to work with.

3 Cut 1½-in/4-cm strips of the felt. Use the Graphic Table Runner Template to cut out the diamonds. Line up the template with parallel sides of the strip and use a rotary cutter to make angled cuts. Cut out a total of 48 diamonds, 16 in each color.

4 Lay out the diamonds in a pattern you like or follow the one pictured (see photo, page 52). You can play with the pieces as if they were tiles. Remember: The pattern is meant to look decon-structed. After you have selected the pattern, take a picture so you can refer to it later. The following directions explain how to piece the table runner that is pictured; it can also be used as a guide if you want to sew the diamonds together in a different pattern.

5 With 1 diamond of each of the 3 colors, sew the 3 diamonds together to create a hexagon using a wide zigzag stitch on your sewing machine, like this: Lay 2 pieces flat, right next to each other, and sew them together using the zigzag stitch through both pieces. Then sew the third piece to the joined pieces, by fitting one of the shallow points into the V created by the joined pieces. Zigzag the abutted edges. Repeat with the other diamonds until you have 16 hexagons.

6 With all the hexagons facing the same direction, start to zigzag the sides of the hexagons together to create strips. For this runner, create 3 separate strips of hexagons: one strip with 3 hexagons, a second strip with 5 hexagons, and a third strip with 6 hexagons. There will be 2 hexagons left, which will be used in Step 7.

7 Place the strip with 5 hexagons on top of the strip of 6, and offset the top strip so that it hangs over the edge of one end of the bottom strip. Abut all the edges that fit together and join them with a zigzag stitch. Place the 3-hexagon strip below the strip of 6, offsetting the smaller strip so it sits toward the left edge of the longer strip. Abut all the edges that fit together and join with a zigzag stitch. Place one of the remaining single hexagons along the top edge of joined pieces, in the second V from the left. Zigzag in place. Then place the last hexagon along the bottom edge of the joined pieces, in the second V from the left, and zigzag in place.

8 Lay the runner on a piece of fusible web, and trace around it. Cut the fusible web slightly smaller than the runner and place it onto the felt for the back of the runner. Then place the pieced runner top over the fusible web, making sure that all of the fusible web is covered and sandwiched between the top (pieced) layer of felt and the backing layer of felt. Following the fusible web instructions, use an iron to fuse the pieces together, taking care not to singe the wool.

9 Use sharp scissors to trim the felt backing to the same size as the pieced runner top.

10 Run a straight stitch along the border of the runner, about ⅛ in/3 mm from the edge.

VARIATIONS

* Make your table runner in one color for a modern, monochromatic look.

* Try making a full-size table runner to cover the length of your table.

* Make smaller versions of this project and use as coasters around your house.

This garland is a great project for using leftover felt pieces. It will remind you of the particular joy that comes from turning what some might call trash into decorative treasure—particularly when it comes to making quick party decorations.

MATERIALS	TOOLS
Scraps of felt 1 to 2 in/2.5 to 5 cm in size, or cut larger pieces of felt down to size	Scissors
	Sewing machine
Sewing thread	
Two ½-in/12-mm plastic circles	

1 Cut the scraps of felt into any shapes you like. We used triangles and squares.

2 With the sewing machine set to straight stitch, feed the felt shapes through the machine, and center the stitching on each shape. Don't cut the thread after each shape, but just keep sewing and leave lengths of thread of varying sizes between the shapes to add interest.

3 Leave long thread tails at each end of the garland of shapes and knot a plastic circle to each end for hanging. Hang wherever you need a little felt flair.

VARIATIONS

* Make longer strands and use to decorate your Christmas tree.

* Use instead of ribbon as an extra special wrap around gifts.

* Make a few strands, attach them together at the ends, and hang your multitiered garland.

JILL COLLIER

PROVO, UTAH

ith three young daughters, Jill has learned to be creative about finding time to make things. "I have to put off my creative time until my girls are asleep at night," she says. Her dedication to her family and her craft stems from how she grew up: Her mother was an amazing seamstress and taught Jill basic sewing skills early on. "I have great memories of the times we spent together doing crafts and sewing, and I'm thankful to have those skills now as an adult," she explains. Recently, Jill started using felt with her pillows and accessories and she fell for the material. "I have a hard time finding home decor and accents that express me fully, so I love to create my own ideas," she says. She often finds inspiration in combining contemporary design with vintage notions. And with felt, she explains, it's also about the structure of the material itself, "which makes for elegant, clean-cut edges that are easy to work with."

"With felt, you don't have to worry about raw edges like you do with other fabrics."

FIND JILL
Jillybeancraft.etsy.com

Soft, pretty, and playful, this pillow is a perfect way to dress up a couch, bed, or chair. Make it in fabrics that coordinate or contrast with your furniture, depending on your preference.

MATERIALS

¾ yd/67 cm medium- to heavy-weight cotton fabric, 44 in/110 cm wide, in a solid color

Sewing thread, in a color that coordinates with your cotton fabric

¼ yd/23 cm wool felt, 20 in/50 cm wide, in 2 coordinating colors

Scraps of wool felt in 2 additional coordinating colors

Sewing thread in colors that coordinate with your felt

1 bag polyester fiberfill

TOOLS

Scissors

Pins

Iron and ironing board

Sewing machine

3-in/7.5-cm Circle Template

2-in/5-cm Circle Template

1½-in/4-cm Circle Template

1-in/2.5-cm Circle Template

Sewing needle

Pencil

Make sure to prewash, dry, and iron your cotton fabric before starting the project.

1 From the cotton fabric, cut 1 rectangle that measures 22 by 14 in/55 by 35.5 cm for the pillow back. Then, cut a second rectangle from the cotton that measures 25 by 14 in/62 by 35.5 cm for the pillow front.

2 Fold five ¼-in/6-mm pleats along the left side of the front piece of the pillow, starting 2½ in/6 cm from the edge, and spaced 1¾ to 2 in/4.5 to 5 cm apart. Pin to hold them in place, and press the pleats down. Use your sewing machine to stitch down each pleat from top to bottom about ⅛ in/3 mm from the folded edge. Complete another line of stitching about ¼ in/6 mm to the right of your first line of stitching. Use a decorative stitch, as pictured (see photo, page 60), if desired, or a straight stitch.

3 Cut out 11 of the 3-in/7.5-cm Circle Template from the felt for the largest poppy piece, alternating between the two coordinating colors. Cut the edges of each petal squiggly rather than perfectly round. Then cut 11 each of the 2-in/5-cm Circle Template and the 1½-in/4-cm Circle Template to make slightly smaller petals. Then cut 11 of the 1-in/2.5-cm Circle Template, alternating between scraps of the two coordinating colors.

4 To form the shape of the poppies, fold each circle in half, then in half again, and stitch together across the folded point of the felt. Repeat with the additional circles. Layer 3 to 4 petals together, with the largest ones at the base, and hand-stitch through the center to form each poppy.

5 Sew the finished poppies to the front piece of the pillow along your stitched-down pleats as shown, using a few hand-stitches through the center of each poppy.

6 Place pillow front and pillow back rectangles atop each other, with right sides together, aligning all edges, and pin. With the sewing machine, use a ½-in/12-mm seam allowance and sew the pillow cover together around the edges, pivoting at each corner. Make sure to leave a 5-in/12-cm opening along the bottom, and backstitch at the beginning and end of the seam. Run a zigzag stitch around the raw edges.

7 Turn the pillow cover right side out, poke out the corners with a pencil eraser, and press the seams flat.

8 Stuff the pillow cover with the fiberfill through the opening on the bottom until it's tightly filled. Hand-stitch the opening closed.

* Play around with using bright colors for the fabric.

* Sew the flowers onto a premade pillow cover to simplify.

* Make more poppies for the face of the pillow for a bigger punch.

Whether for a night out, a special event, or just a place to hold your wallet, keys, and phone for a coffee date with a friend, this attractive clutch can go places.

MATERIALS

½ yd/46 cm heavy-weight cotton or linen canvas fabric, 54 in/137 cm wide, in a color of your choice

½ yd/46 cm medium-weight fusible interfacing, 20 in/51 cm wide, in coordinating color

¼ yd/23 cm wool felt, 20 in/50 cm wide, in 3 coordinating colors

Sewing thread, in coordinating color

Scissors

Rotary cutter (optional)

Cutting mat (optional)

Clear gridded ruler

Iron and ironing board

3-in/7.5-cm Circle Template

2-in/5-cm Circle Template

1½ -in/4-cm Circle Template

TOOLS

1-in/2.5-cm Circle Template

Sewing needle

Glue gun and glue sticks (optional)

4½-in/11-cm-diameter (approximately) circular object like the rim of a drinking glass or roll of masking tape

Pins

Sewing machine

Make sure to prewash, dry, and iron your cotton or linen fabric before starting the project.

The finished clutch should measure approximately 12 by 6½ in/30.5 by 16.5 cm.

Note: The front and back pieces of the clutch are the pieces that need the interfacing, as well as the front flap.

Make the Clutch Pieces

1 Cut the following pieces of the clutch fabric and interfacing using scissors or a rotary cutter and mat:

Clutch Body
Four 13-by-7½-in/33-by-19-cm rectangles of fabric

Two 13-by-7½-in/33-by-19-cm rectangles of interfacing

Front Flap
Two 13-by-5½-in/33-by-14-cm rectangles of fabric

One 13-by-5½-in/33-by-14-cm rectangle of interfacing

2 Iron on the interfacing: For the clutch body, iron 1 piece of the same-size interfacing to each of the wrong sides of 2 pieces of fabric. Then for the front flap, iron 1 piece of the same-size interfacing to the wrong side of 1 piece of the flap fabric.

Make the Flowers

1 For each flower, use the 3 templates (as follows) to cut flower petal circles from the felt in the three colors of your choosing:

One from the 3-in/7.5-cm Circle Template

Four to five from the 2-in/5-cm Circle Template

Four to five from the 1½-in/4-cm Circle Template

Five to six from the 1-in/2.5-cm Circle Template

2 To make a flower, place your largest circle (3 in/7.5 cm) down as the base. Next, fold one 2-in/5-cm circle in half and secure it to an outer edge of the base by hand-stitching (or hot gluing) it along the folded edge. The curved part of the petal should face out.

3 Continue working with your 2-in/5-cm circles (per Step 2) to add slightly overlapping petals around the outer edge of the base.

4 Repeat Steps 2 and 3 using the 1½-in/4-cm circles as smaller petals, layering the folded petals on top of the layer that you just put down. Secure as you go along with hand-stitches or hot glue.

5 Then, repeat Steps 2 and 3 using the 1-in/2.5-cm circles, layering these even smaller folded petals on top of the layer that you just put down. Secure as you go with hand-stitches or hot glue. This completes one flower.

6 Continue making flowers, varying the size slightly if you like (as pictured in the photos of the sample clutch, which has 13 flowers), until you have enough to fill the front of the flap.

Complete the Front Flap

1 Hand-stitch through each flower's center to secure it to the front flap and the interfacing. Center the flowers lengthwise along the flap and close together.

2 Place the right sides of the 2 front flap pieces together (1 piece with interfacing, 1 without). Trim 2 rounded corners on 1 lengthwise edge using your circular object (so the flap that is visible on the front of the clutch will have slightly rounded edges). Pin the pieces together, and with the sewing machine, sew together using a ¼-in/6-mm seam allowance, leaving the bottom edge open.

3 Carefully turn the flap right side out by pulling the right sides through. Press the seams flat. Hand-stitch the hole closed using a whipstitch, and with the sewing machine, topstitch around the 3 finished sides of the flap ¼-in/6-mm from the edge.

Complete the Body

1 Stack 1 of the fabric pieces with interfacing with 1 of the fabric pieces without interfacing, right sides together. Pin together. Repeat with the remaining 2 pieces of fabric. Trim 2 rounded corners on each stack so the bottom of the clutch has corners that match the bottom of the front flap.

2 Stitch each stack together using a ¼-in/6-mm seam allowance, leaving a 5-in/10-cm opening along the bottom.

3 Carefully turn each side of the body right side out by pulling the right sides through the opening. Whipstitch the hole closed. Press.

4 Pin 3 sides of the body together, matching up the rounded corners of the front and back on the bottom, and leaving the top unpinned to be the opening of the purse. Use a ¼-in/6-mm seam allowance to topstitch together.

Complete the Clutch

1 Pin the bottom of the flap to the back side of the body of the clutch. The flap should face the back side of the clutch with the rounded corners on the flap at the top. Overlap the finished seams, pin together, and sew to join. Press the seam to encourage the flap to fold over.

* Add a snap closure to your clutch.

* Make the clutch smaller to fit just your evening essentials.

* Make the flowers in all the same color for a monochromatic look.

KASIA PIECYK

LODZ, POLAND

asia says, "I learned to craft with felt together with my sister, Ania, with whom I share the passion of creating handmade accessories. It seemed like we couldn't find items that fully met our expectations, so we started experimenting with various materials and settled on felt as our favorite." Growing up, Kasia was encouraged to craft and be creative: "My grandmother knitted beautiful scarves and sweaters, as well as cross-stitched," she says. "I think my parents are proud that [my sister and I] take the time to create things that are beautiful and unique." Armed with this legacy, Kasia sees herself as a natural crafter. Her work is cheerful and eclectic, simple and modern—features that she says come from paying close attention to the colorful world around her. Her straightforward approach is partly why she loves working with felt—she can cut it, sew it, and glue pieces together any way that she likes to create her gorgeous accessories.

"I attempt to make attractive but useful items that I would want to buy and wear, but mostly, what I do is a way of living, an inseparable part of my life."

FIND KASIA
Piecykspieces.etsy.com

With their intricate spiral layers and elegant final appearance, you'll be surprised at how easy these earrings are to make. Whip up a pair for a friend, and be sure to make some for yourself while you're at it.

MATERIALS

Two 9-by-12-in/23-by-30.5-cm sheets of wool felt, in 2 colors of your choosing

Fabric glue

1½ ft/46 cm nylon-coated stainless steel beading wire (0.018-in/0.5-mm diameter)

2 earring wires

2 crimp beads

TOOLS

Rotary cutter

Cutting mat

Ruler

Toothpick

Wire cutters

Embroidery needle

Crimping pliers

1 With a rotary cutter, cutting mat, and ruler, cut the felt into long narrow strips approximately ³/₈ in/1 cm wide. You will need approximately 4 strips of the main color and 2 strips of the second color.

2 With the second color, roll 1 of the strips tightly into a spiral and apply a bit of fabric glue at the end to secure. Use a toothpick to be precise with your glue placement. Then take 1 strip of the main color and wrap it around the first spiral, and glue the end in place to secure. You now have one 2-color spiral.

3 With the main color, roll a second strip tightly into a spiral and apply a bit of glue at the end to secure. You should now have two spiral circles of different sizes.

4 With wire cutters, cut an approximately 8-in/20-cm length of the beading wire, and thread the embroidery needle with the wire. Stack the two felt spirals, one above the other, as pictured (see photo, page 70), with the larger one on the bottom. Starting from the bottom, pull the needle through the diameter of both circles, leaving a few inches of exposed wire at the bottom.

5 With the needle through both circles, lace one of the earring wires over the wire. Then pull the needle back through both circles, leaving a loop of wire about ½ in/12 mm long at the top. (Or simply pry the earring wire open slightly, place over the wire, and close to secure.)

6 Put 1 crimp bead around both ends of the wire, close to the bottom of the larger circle, then pinch the bead with the crimping pliers to secure the wire ends. Cut off any excess wire with wire cutters.

7 Repeat Steps 2–6 for the second earring.

VARIATIONS

* Make smaller spirals and use three or four per earring for a different look.

* Stick to one color to make this project monochromatic.

* Simplify by using just one spiral per earring.

A soft and delicate necklace that packs a large punch of pretty, this is one accessory that will dress you up without weighing down your neck. Tie the bow as large or small as you like, depending on your mood.

MATERIALS

Four 9-by-12-in/23-by-30.5-cm sheets of felt, in 4 different colors

Fabric glue

1 yd/1 m nylon-coated stainless steel beading wire (0.018-in/0.5-mm diameter)

2 crimp beads

1 yd/1 m ribbon (½ in/12 mm wide)

TOOLS

Rotary cutter

Cutting mat

Ruler

Toothpick

Embroidery needle

Wire cutters

Crimping pliers

1 With a rotary cutter, cutting mat, and ruler, cut the felt into long narrow strips approximately ⅜ in/1 cm wide. You will need approximately 2 strips for each of the small circles, 3 to 4 strips for the medium circles, and 5 to 6 strips for the large circle.

2 Start with 1 strip and roll it tightly into a spiral. Once the center of the spiral is formed, take a second strip in a different color and roll it around the first strip until you reach the end of the strip. Apply a bit of fabric glue at the very end of the strip to secure. Use a toothpick to be precise with your glue placement. Stop here for the small circles. For the larger circles, continue adding more strips in the same colors, until the circles reach the correct diameter. For this necklace, make 10 approximately 1-in-/2.5-cm-diameter circles, 2 approximately 1¼-in-/3.25-cm-diameter circles, and 1 approximately 1½-in-/4-cm-diameter circle. The largest circle will be in the center, with the 2 slightly larger ones on either side of it. Finish the arrangement with 5 of the smallest circles on each side.

3 Thread the needle with the beading wire. Starting at one end of the felt circle arrangement, pull the needle through the diameter of each of the circles, leaving approximately 3 in/7.5 cm of exposed wire at the end.

4 Thread a crimp bead onto the needle, then turn the needle around and thread it back through the crimp bead, leaving a loop about ½ in/12 mm long. Then pull the needle back through the last circle. Pinch the crimp bead with the crimping pliers to secure the loop. Cut off any excess wire that extends past the last circle (between the last 2 end circles, not the loop).

5 Gently push all the circles together, so they are snug and no wire peeks between them.

6 On the end without the loop, repeat Step 4 to create a second looped end.

7 Knot the ends of your ribbon to prevent fraying. Then lace each end through the loops, and tie on with a bow.

VARIATIONS

* Use silver chain or a length of leather in place of ribbon.

* Make the spirals smaller for a more delicate necklace.

* Vary the colors of the spirals for a more vibrant necklace.

JEN FITZSIMMONS

MELVILLE, NEW YORK

When she recently saw some gorgeous pincushions made of felt, Jen decided to play with the material. "I just dove right in!" she exclaims. After her day job, she reserves evenings at home for fun, and loves "getting settled in, working with colors and textures." For Jen, having two distinct parts of her day offers a necessary balance. "I was never a kid who would just sit and watch TV. I was always doing something and was completely obsessed with building with Legos," she remembers. Jen has developed a creative style that bridges the modern and the classic—clean lines and pops of color, achieved through the tactile qualities and texture of felt. "Felt is very forgiving and versatile; it's simple and yet you can use it in intricate ways," she says. Inspired by life around her, Jen takes creative energy from things as diverse as a gorgeous blouse and a beautifully decorated room, proving that a muse can be found anywhere if you're on the lookout for it.

"I love to try any idea that pops into my head, and it may work or it may not, but more often than not, it spins off into something awesome! You never know unless you give it a shot."

FIND JEN

Itz-fitz.com   ItzFitz.etsy.com   Facebook.com/ItzFitzShop

Your door will be the prettiest on the block if you decorate it with one of these stunning wreaths. Choose your colors based on the season you're celebrating, or just choose what makes you happy when you return home each day.

MATERIALS

One 12-in/30.5-cm straw wreath form

1 skein of yarn, approximately 364 yds/ 333 m, in a color of your choosing

200 to 300 yd/183 to 274 m worsted- weight yarn, in a color or colors of your choosing

Three to four 9-by-12-in/23-by-30.5-cm sheets of wool felt, in 2 shades of the same color

One wreath hook (available at most craft or hardware stores)

TOOLS

Disappearing fabric marker

Scissors

Glue gun and glue sticks

1 Secure an end of the yarn to the wreath form by holding it in place, and start wrapping the yarn around the form, covering the loose end. Continue wrapping the wreath form with yarn until it is completely covered. Tuck in any loose ends. If you want a striped wreath, wrap yarn in alternating colors to get that look.

2 For the flowers, using a disappearing fabric marker, draw circles on the felt of many different sizes, from about ¾ in/ 2 cm to 2 ½ in/6 cm. The sizes can vary, since you will be making flowers of different sizes, as pictured (see photo, page 78). The larger flowers need 7 to 10 circles each and the smaller flowers need 1 to 3 circles.

3 To make a flower, start with 1 of the smallest felt circles. Roll it into a tube and use hot glue to secure it to make the center of the flower. Take another small circle of felt, wrap it around the center circle, and glue it in place. You will want to mimic the interior petals of a rose. Continue wrapping felt circles around the center ones, using larger circles each time, until you reach the size of flower that you want. As you go, cut off any excess felt on the bottom of the flower, because the bottom needs to be flat so it can be secured to the wreath. Make as many flowers as you want in varying sizes.

4 Determine where you'd like to place your flowers on the wreath and glue them in place, securely.

5 Hang your wreath on your front door using a wreath hook.

VARIATIONS

* Vary the size of your wreath by choosing a different size form.

* Make the wreath more mod by skipping the flowers altogether.

* Use more flowers in varying sizes to create a spray of buds across one side of the wreath.

Wrapping packages is a platform for showing off a little creativity. For turning the outside of a box into as much of a gift as what's inside, try dressing it up with a homemade bow that the recipient can reuse for years to come.

MATERIALS

One 9-by-12-in/23-by-30.5-cm sheet of wool felt for 1 bow

TOOLS

Ruler

Rotary cutter

Cutting mat

Glue gun and glue sticks

1 To make one bow, measure and cut the felt into several strips using the ruler, rotary cutter, and cutting mat:

3 strips 9 by 1 in/23 by 2.5 cm

2 strips 8 by ¾ in/20 by 2 cm

2 strips 7 by ¾ in/17 by 2 cm

1 strip 3 ¾ by ¾ in/9.5 by 2 cm (for middle loop)

1 strip 3 by ⅝ in/7.5 cm by 16 mm (for back loop)

2 Twist each of the 7 longest strips into a figure-8 shape, with the ends meeting in the middle. Using hot glue, glue the ends together in the middle to secure this shape.

3 Starting with one of the largest twisted strips on the bottom, stack another of the large twisted strips on top and perpendicular to the first one. Glue the middle of these 2 twisted strips together. Continue stacking the twisted loop pieces, in this fashion, until all 7 of the twisted loops are glued together, from largest at the bottom to smallest at the top.

4 Using the strip cut for the middle loop, don't twist this one, but shape into a loop and place it on the top of the smallest twisted loop. You may need to play with the size of this loop a bit to fit in the middle of the smallest twisted loop. Once you are happy with the size of the middle loop, glue the ends in place. You now have a pretty bow!

5 Place the smallest strip on the bottom of the bow, and form a loop. Glue the ends in place. Use this loop to attach the bow to the package, by either threading a piece of ribbon, yarn, or twine through the loop or simply taping the loop to the package.

VARIATIONS

* Make a handful of bows and use them to decorate a Christmas tree.

* Make the bows in whichever color suits the occasion or the gift that you are giving.

* Try adjusting the length and thickness of the strips to make mini bows for smaller gifts.

SANDIE ZIMMERMAN

INDIANAPOLIS, INDIANA

arried to her high school sweetheart, Sandie has a home life that is a creative person's ideal: "We live a happy, cozy life in our yellow house with a white porch. My husband thinks everything I make is beautiful even if it isn't. We have a son and a daughter who don't think twice when their mom stitches at the beach, and they've learned to watch out when cuddling next to me so they don't get poked with a needle." Sandie grew up in the Midwest and developed a fondness for such seemingly old-fashioned techniques as embroidery, which her mom taught her when she was in elementary school. "Often when I stitch, I think about how that moment, when she took the time to sit by my side and teach me something that she enjoyed, has made such a big impact on my life," she says. Sandie transforms her inspirations into skillfully executed crafts made of felt. "I like how the more you handle felt, the softer it gets."

"Felt is so forgiving. You can pull out a big mess of stitches and never notice where you messed up."

Since the foundation of this sophisticated fascinator (or fancy hair accessory) provides the backdrop for the final aesthetic, go for the good stuff—100 percent wool felt, that is. Wear it slightly off center, with your hair down or pulled back into a low bun, for an instant style upgrade.

MATERIALS

One 6-by-6-in/15-by-15-cm piece of charcoal gray wool felt

4 skeins DMC embroidery thread, 1 each in light yellow (834), gray (413), aloe green (502), and light gray (648)

Fabric glue

One ¼-in/6-mm-wide black elastic headband (available at most drugstores)

TOOLS

2¾-in/7-cm Circle Template

Disappearing fabric marker or transfer paper

Pinking shears

2-in/5-cm Circle Template

Helen Fascinator Pattern

Embroidery needle

Scissors

Note: All embroidery and sewing for this project is done with 3 strands of the embroidery thread.

1 With the 2¾-in/7-cm Circle Template, trace 2 circles onto the felt and and cut them out with pinking shears. Then with the 2-in/5-cm Circle Template, trace 1 circle from the felt and cut it out with pinking shears.

2 Using the Helen Fascinator Pattern as a guide, draw the design on the 2-in/5-cm circle of felt with the disappearing fabric marker or transfer paper.

3 With the lightest 3 colors of embroidery thread, embroider the design using detached chain or lazy daisy stitches (see photo for thread color placement). Feel free to improvise your stitches if you have a style of embroidery or a stitch that you particularly enjoy.

4 Place the stitched circle on top of one of the 2¾-in/7-cm felt circles and lightly glue them together with fabric glue. Allow the glue to dry. With the gray embroidery thread, sew a running stitch ⅛ in/3 mm from the edge, around the smaller circle and through both layers.

5 Sandwich the black elastic headband between the remaining large circle and the back of your fascinator. Glue together with fabric glue and allow to dry completely before wearing.

VARIATIONS

✳ Use a thick piece of ribbon or leather in place of the elastic to change the look.

✳ Add extra felt embellishments and adhere as you're stitching the design.

✳ Make two smaller circles and wear both on one headband to vary the design.

Sweet stitches provide a tactile adornment on this felt headband. The adjustable tie-on design will ensure that you can wear it with braids or with a ponytail (no headache involved) with a sweet bow at the base of your neck.

MATERIALS

One 12-by-4-in/30.5-by-10-cm piece of wool felt, in aloe green

4 skeins of DMC embroidery thread, 1 each in light yellow (834), gray (413), aloe green (502), light gray (648)

1⅓ yd/1.3 m black grosgrain ribbon, 1 in/2.5 cm wide

TOOLS

Ruler

Scissors

Sharon Headband Pattern

Disappearing fabric marker or transfer paper

Embroidery needle

Note: All embroidery and sewing for this project is done with 3 strands of the embroidery thread.

1 Measure and cut out 2 rectangles, 11 by 1¾ in/28 by 4.5 cm each, from the felt.

2 Using the Sharon Headband Pattern as a guide, draw the design on one of the felt rectangles with disappearing fabric marker or transfer paper.

3 With the yellow and 2 gray colors of embroidery thread, embroider the design using lazy daisy stitches, cross-stitches, and straight stitches (see photo for thread color placement). Feel free to improvise your stitches if you have a style of embroidery or stitch that you particularly enjoy.

4 Cut the ribbon in half. Trim each corner of the felt rectangle, so each of the 2 ends is tapered like a triangle. Pin together both felt rectangle pieces with ½ in/12 mm of the ribbon sandwiched between each tapered end.

5 With aloe green embroidery thread, sew the 2 felt pieces together with a running stitch ⅛ in/3 mm from the edge, making sure to go through all layers and catch the ribbon in the stitching. Tie the headband around your head to wear it.

VARIATIONS

* Hold the headband onto your head and have a friend measure the open space between the ends. Subtract ½ in/ 12 mm from that amount, cut a piece of elastic to your length, and sew on to either end for a bowless closure.

* Leave the ribbon ends much longer and turn the headband into a belt (and even extend the length of the felt if you wish).

* Change up the colors of the felt and/ or the ribbon according to your mood.

JEANIE LAI

PORTLAND, OREGON

When Jeanie was little, she wanted to become a fashion designer, but she found her way into a career as an architectural designer. Then, she says, "A few years back, I was browsing around at Kinokuniya, a local Japanese bookstore, and came across some Japanese craft books about felting." And she soon took a felt crafting class at a local knitting shop. "After the class, I started making felt jewelry, first for myself, and soon I was selling necklaces to friends and coworkers," she continues. "Designing buildings requires a more collaborative process and it can take years before you see your work come to life. Felting is a way for me to create more immediate and tangible things all on my own," she says. Her inspiration comes from an interest in mid-twentieth-century furniture and artifacts and the openness of the craft scene in Portland. Plus, there's the material itself: "This simple, honest material has endless design possibilities."

"I love felt for its inherent tactile qualities; it's a perfect material to lend warmth to my modern minimal aesthetic."

FIND JEANIE
Moufelt.com   Moufelt.etsy.com

This intricate necklace takes some patience to craft, but the steps are soothingly repetitive. So turn on some of your favorite music and make an afternoon of it. (The picture shows three versions of the necklace, in shades of red, gray, and green.)

MATERIALS

Three 9-by-12-in/23-by-30.5-cm sheet of wool felt (1.5 mm thick), in 3 shades of one color

2½ ft/76 cm of nylon-coated stainless steel beading wire (0.018-in/0.5-mm diameter)

2 crimp beads

Clasp of your choice

TOOLS

Die cutter (such as Squeeze by QuicKutz), or scissors

1-in/2.5-cm-diameter Circle Template, or die

½-in/12-mm-diameter Circle Template, or die

Pencil

Wire cutters

Embroidery needle

Crimping pliers

If you don't have a die cutter, which makes very quick work of this project, make an appropriately sized circle template out of cardstock and draw each circle onto the felt using a pencil. Then simply cut out each circle as indicated.

Make the Ruffles

1 With the 1-in/2.5-cm Circle Template or circle die, cut out 30 felt circles in each of the 3 colors for a total of 90 circles.

2 With the ½-in/12-mm Circle Template or circle die, cut out 30 felt circles in each of the 3 colors for a total of 90 circles.

3 Make a set of the felt circles with the bigger circle on the bottom, in this order (using the gray necklace, pictured, as the example): Color set A: charcoal (1 in/2.5 cm), medium gray (½ in/12 mm).

4 Make a second set of felt circles with the bigger circle on the bottom, in this order: Color set B: light gray (1 in/2.5 cm), charcoal (½ in/12 mm).

5 Make a third set of felt circles with the bigger circle on the bottom in this order: Color set C: medium gray (1 in/2.5 cm), light gray (½ in/12 mm). You should have a total of 90 sets.

Make the Necklace

1 With the wire cutter, cut off a 27-in/67-cm length of beading wire.

2 Thread the wire through the embroidery needle and fold over one end of the wire about ½ in/12 mm, so the felt circles won't fall off once they are threaded on.

3 Gently fold each set of felt circles in half with your fingers to create a ruffle. Thread both circles of each pair in a set at the same time onto the needle, slightly off center. Start with color set A, then B, and then C, threading each set onto the wire. Repeat until all 90 sets are threaded onto the wire. Remove the embroidery needle.

4 Cut the wire to 25 in/62 cm. Then thread 1 crimp bead and 1 side of the clasp on one end of the wire. Draw the wire back through the crimp bead, so the clasp is held in place by a loop. With the crimping pliers, crimp the bead to hold the wire in place. Cut off any extra wire. Repeat on other side of necklace with the remaining crimp bead and the other half of the clasp.

* Make the necklace shorter, turning it into a bracelet (measure a bracelet you love for an approximate length for the wire).

* Mix and match the felt colors as you like.

* Make a second strand either slightly longer or slightly shorter, for a two-strand necklace.

Simple yet stunning, these earrings will dress up any outfit. Be sure to buy high-quality earring wires to ensure that they are safe to wear and will last for years to come.

MATERIALS

One 4-by-4-in/10-by-10-cm piece of wool felt, 1.5 mm thick, in a color of your choice

2 sterling silver head pins (2 in/ 5 cm long)

2 earring wires of your choice

TOOLS

Hand punch that makes ¼-in/ 6-mm-diameter circles

Bead reamer

Round-nose pliers

Flat-nose pliers

1 With the hand punch, cut out 16 circles from the felt.

2 Divide the circles into 2 sets of 8 and stack them up as best as you can. Using the bead reamer, punch a hole into all 8 circles. Then remove the circles from the reamer and thread them onto a head pin. Repeat with the second set of circles.

3 Push the felt circles to the bottom of each head pin. With the round-nose pliers, make a loop at the top of each head pin.

4 With the flat-nose pliers, loosen the loop of the earring wire and hook on the head pin.

5 Repeat Step 4 for the second earring to complete your pair.

VARIATIONS

* Use more than one color of felt in each earring for a more vibrant look.

* Make the earrings longer for a more dramatic accessory.

* Try this method of stacking small felt circles to craft yourself a nifty necklace.

LAURA HOWARD

GLOUCESTER, ENGLAND

As a self-employed crafty lady, Laura has her hands full—literally—with making things. "I make hand-stitched felt accessories, sell craft supplies, and design crafty projects for books and magazines," she says. Laura is the author of *Super-Cute Felt* and says, "It's wonderful being able to rearrange my schedule if I get the sudden itch to work on a new project." As a child, Laura loved to make things, especially those that involved cutting and sticking. "My parents bought me a small sewing machine and I think they were a bit disappointed when it sat gathering dust—I preferred making little hand-sewn things, and felt was the perfect material to use for stuff like hats for dolls, bookmarks, and bracelets," she recalls. After university, Laura used crafting as a way to cheer her spirits during an illness, and soon became completely obsessed with felt. "I love the huge range of felt colors available—my felt stash is the sewing equivalent of having a big box of colored pencils, one in every color of the rainbow."

"I love the challenge of translating a real, lovely thing like a bird or a flower into something small and felt-y."

FIND LAURA

Lupinhandmade.com   Bugsandfishes.blogspot.com   Twitter.com/bugsandfishes
Facebook.com/lupinhandmade

The mosaic design on this pincushion is a great way to use up small pieces of felt left over from other projects. Make the pincushion in your favorite colors, or make a rainbow mosaic with each diamond in a different color.

MATERIALS

One 9-by-12 in/23-by-30.5-cm sheet of gray wool felt

Six 2-by-2-in/5-by-5-cm pieces wool felt, in 6 different colors

Sewing thread, in coordinating colors

Felt/fabric scraps or polyfill, for stuffing

TOOLS

Pincushion Template

Disappearing fabric marker

Scissors

Ruler

1 sheet of paper

Sewing needle

1 Using the circle in the Pincushion Template, trace 2 circles onto the gray felt, and cut them out; these will be for the top and bottom of the pincushion. Then cut out a 12-by-1¾-in/30.5-by-4.5-cm rectangle of gray felt, for the sides of the pincushion.

2 Using the diamond shape in the Pincushion Template, trace 4 diamonds onto each of the 6 shades of felt and cut them out, for a total of 24 diamonds. Be sure to cut the diamonds as accurately as possible to ensure that the mosaic design fits together properly.

3 Place the diamonds on a sheet of paper and arrange them in different compositions until you're happy with the colorful design.

4 Transfer and sew the diamonds from the paper to one of the gray felt circles, starting with the 8 center diamonds. Use matching thread and small whipstitches to sew each diamond in place. Take care to make the points of the diamonds meet neatly. This piece will be the top of the pincushion.

5 With matching thread, sew the top circle and rectangle together, using small whipstitches, turning the circle gradually as you sew the edges together. When you've sewn all the way around the circle, trim any excess felt from the rectangle, so that the short ends abut each other. Sew up the side seam of the pincushion with small whipstitches. Then sew the bottom felt circle in place with small whipstitches, stopping three-quarters of the way around to leave an opening for stuffing. Don't cut the thread.

6 Stuff the pincushion with felt/fabric scraps or polyfill. Use your fingers to press the stuffing into the pincushion until it's firmly and evenly stuffed and has a nice shape.

7 Whipstitch the opening closed, knot the thread, and cut off any excess.

VARIATIONS

* Use the mosaic design to make a brooch.

* Enlarge the mosaic design for decorating a pillow.

* Embroider a loved one's name onto the bottom circle of the pincushion and give it as a gift.

This sparkly dragonfly pennant is embellished with sequins, beads, and shimmering metallic embroidery floss.

MATERIALS

Three 9-by-9-in/23-by-23-cm sheets of wool felt, olive green

One 6-by-6-in/15-by-15-cm piece of wool felt, turquoise

Two 9-by-9-in/23-by-23-cm sheets of wool felt, light turquoise

Sewing thread, in matching colors

2 skeins of metallic embroidery floss, 1 each in gold and turquoise

26 turquoise sequins

42 turquoise bugle beads

$5/8$-yd/57-cm rickrack, $1/4$ in/ 6 mm wide, in light blue

TOOLS

Dragonfly Pennant Template

Scissors

Pins

Sewing needle

Large embroidery needle

In the Dragonfly Pennant Template, the wing templates are for the left wings. Make sure to flip them over to use them for the right wings.

1 With the Dragonfly Pennant Template, trace and cut out the following pieces for each dragonfly:

1 dragonfly body in olive green felt

1 left and 1 right dragonfly top wing in turquoise felt

1 left and 1 right dragonfly bottom wing in turquoise felt

1 full dragonfly in light turquoise felt

2 Place the light turquoise dragonfly piece on a piece of olive green felt, leaving enough room to cut a narrow border around the edge. Arrange the body and wing pieces on top and pin them in position through all layers of felt.

3 With matching thread and using the sewing needle and a small whipstitch, sew the body and wing pieces in place, through all layers. Remove the pins as you finish sewing each piece. Start with the body piece then sew the wings one by one, taking care to sew the shapes together exactly where they meet.

4 Cut away the olive green felt around the dragonfly shape, leaving an ⅛-in/3-mm border of olive green felt.

5 Cut a length of gold metallic embroidery floss, and divide the strands so you're just using 3 strands. Thread the embroidery needle, sew a line of running stitch around the edges of the 4 wing shapes, taking care not to pull the stitches too tight (which could pucker the felt). Sew back along the line between the gaps to create a continuous line of stitching.

Note: You could use a backstitch instead, but sewing twice around in running stitch uses less floss and the strands get less tangled. Metallic embroidery floss can be a bit tricky to work with because the strands tend to separate and tangle more easily than standard floss. For ease of stitching with metallic thread, cut shorter lengths than you'd normally use, and take your time stitching.

6 Sew the wing decorations. Whichever decoration you're applying, remember to make the wings mirror images of each other:

Sequins
Position several turquoise sequins in a pleasing arrangement, then sew them in place on the wings, one by one, using the sewing needle, turquoise thread, and 3 stitches per sequin.

Embroidery
Use the embroidery needle and the metallic turquoise embroidery floss (separating half the strands as in Step 5) to backstitch a zigzag line along each wing, as pictured (see photo, page 109).

Beads
Sew turquoise bugle beads along each wing to create a pattern. Use the sewing needle and a double strand of turquoise sewing thread and 1 stitch per bead.

7 Pin the completed dragonfly to a piece of olive green felt, and use it as a template to cut out a matching shape (for the backing of the dragonfly so that your stitches are hidden). Remove the pin and set aside the backing piece. Repeat Steps 2–7 for each dragonfly.

8 Turn your dragonflies over and trim any excess threads at the back. With the sewing needle and olive green sewing thread and starting with the bottom dragonfly, whipstitch the rickrack in place, down the center of the dragonfly bodies, as pictured (see photo, page 109). Be sure to sew into only 1 layer of felt, so the stitching isn't visible on the front of the dragonfly. Leave about a 2-in/5-cm gap between each dragonfly. At the top, fold over the remaining rickrack to create a loop for hanging, and tack the raw edge of the rickrack in place.

9 Pin a dragonfly backing piece (that was cut in Step 7) to the back of each dragonfly. Sew the layers together with the sewing needle and matching olive green thread and use a running stitch. You will want your running stitch to be along the edge of the light turquoise layer so your stitching is largely hidden. Remove the pins as you sew and finish your stitching neatly on the back.

10 Hang the pennant from a small hook on the wall out of direct sunlight to avoid fading and out of reach of small children.

VARIATIONS

* For an extra hit of shimmer you could use narrow ribbon instead of rickrack, and thread beads between the dragonflies.

* For a stunning presentation, make two more strands of dragonflies and hang them together, as pictured (see photo, page 108).

* Make individual dragonflies and use or give them as ornaments.

* Make enough dragonflies to sew onto a garland and use it to decorate a room in your house for a bit of whimsy.

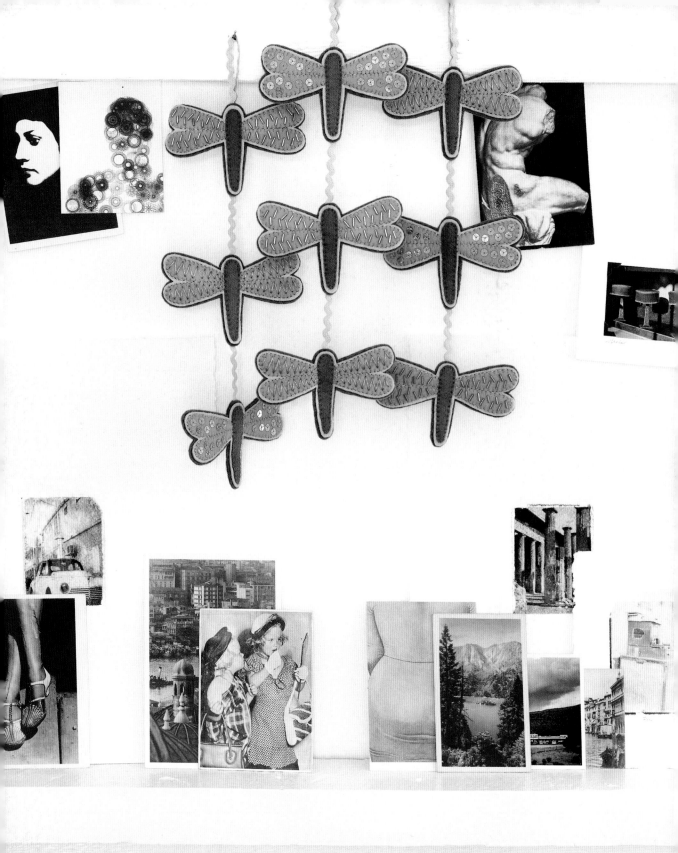

NICOLE FRANKE

GILBERT, ARIZONA

icole's craft business started just a few years ago after her second son was born. "I had the desire to start a business from home. I just needed to find my craft," she explains. "One day, I wanted to try to make a fresh, modern wreath for my house using felt flowers. I started to play and practice and I eventually created one for myself, and then began making them as gifts. I immediately knew I had discovered my niche," she says. "I absolutely love what I do," she continues. "It makes me happy to be able to stay home with my boys and make pretty things." Her pretty, modern, and sophisticated takes on wedding bouquets are a big hit. "I love being able to create beautiful unique pieces for a bride's big day and know they will be something to treasure for years after the occasion has passed." That collectible idea is tied to her material of choice, felt.

"Wool felt is soft and smooth and doesn't unravel. When you're crafting felt flowers, you want something thick and sturdy, so synthetic felt won't do."

FIND NICOLE
Handmadecolectibles.etsy.com

Perfect for a DIY wedding, this bouquet is an instant collectible. It can be made far in advance of the big day and makes a memorable accent for any occasion. A felt rose bouquet is also a fuss-free way to keep a dose of spring on your counter or kitchen table all year long.

MATERIALS

Twelve 9-by-12-in/23-by-30.5-cm sheets of wool felt (1 per rose), in orange, tangerine, gold, mustard, magenta, rose, or in colors of your choice

Two to three 9-by-12-in/23-by-30.5-cm sheets of wool felt for the leaves, in moss green

Twelve 15-in/38-cm green florist wood stakes

One hand-tied bouquet holder (like the BRAVO bouquet holders available at craft stores or Tcgfloral.com)

Spool of 1½-in-/4-cm-wide ribbon, preferably grosgrain, in coordinating color

One faux pearl–head pin

TOOLS

Ruler

Disappearing fabric marker

Scissors

Glue gun and glue sticks

Deckle-edge scissors (optional)

Pliers

1 Using the ruler and disappearing fabric marker, divide the sheets of felt being used for the roses into long strips of varying widths between 2 to 3 in/5 to 7.5 cm wide. Then cut out with scissors.

2 From the strips, cut half-moon shapes for the rose petals, ranging in size from small to large. You'll want to end up with 5–10 small petals, 5–10 medium petals, 5–10 large petals.

Note: You may not end up using every petal, but it's better to have a few extra than to run out.

3 Take a small petal, dab a dot of hot glue on the base, and roll it tightly together to form a bud. Continue dabbing glue onto petals and attaching them around the first bud, moving from small to large petals as you work outward until you reach the size of rose you want.

4 Trace and cut out 3–5 leaf shapes for each rose, using deckle-edge scissors, if desired, for a toothed edge.

5 Hot glue a wooden stake to the bottom of your rose to create a stem. Hold the stake in place until the glue is completely dry. Glue felt leaves around the base of the rose to cover the glued bottom. Repeat Steps 2–5 until you have 12 roses, varying the sizes of the roses slightly to make a natural-looking bouquet.

6 Cut the wooden stakes in half with the pliers, reserving the cut ends. Starting at the center, add one rose at a time to the bouquet holder. Glue the stems in place in the foam of the bouquet holder as you go so they are secure.

7 When all roses are in place, glue on more leaves to cover all of the stems, foam, and any excess hot glue.

8 Put a dab of glue on the top of one side of the holder and start wrapping your ribbon around, slightly overlapping the ribbon as you work downward. When the holder is completely wrapped with the ribbon, fold the raw edge of the ribbon under and secure with the faux pearl–head pin.

9 Tuck the reserved stake ends from Step 6 into the base of the bouquet holder, and glue them in place so they are secure, to complete your bouquet.

VARIATIONS

∗ Make the roses all the same color for a sophisticated, monochromatic look.

∗ Make a mini bouquet for a flower girl or junior bridesmaid.

∗ Use strips of a favorite fabric in place of ribbon to adorn the holder.

Give your man a touch of felt fancy on the big day with these handmade boutonnieres. No wedding in sight? Transform the project by calling it a corsage and wear it on a plain sweater to brighten up any day of the week.

MATERIALS

Three 9-by-12-in/23-by-30.5-cm sheets of wool felt, in orange, magenta, and moss green, or in colors of your choice

9-in/23-cm of grapevine wire

Small spool of thin twine

1 faux pearl–head pin

TOOLS

Scissors

Ruler

Disappearing fabric marker

Glue gun and glue sticks

Wire cutters

Note: Finished size of roses is approximately 2 in/5 cm in diameter.

1 Using the ruler and disappearing fabric marker, divide the sheets of felt being used for the roses into long strips, varying the width of the strips so that they measure between 2 to 3 in/5 to 7.5 cm wide. Then cut out with scissors.

2 From the strips, cut half-moon shapes, ranging in size from small to large. These will form your rose petals. You'll want to end up with 5–10 small petals, 5–10 medium petals, 5–10 large petals per rose.

Note: You may not end up using every single petal, but it's better to have a few extra than to run out.

3 Take a small petal, dab a dot of hot glue on the base, and roll it tightly together to form a bud. Continue dabbing glue onto the petals and attaching them around the first bud, moving from small to large as you work outward. Stop when the rose reaches approximately three-quarters the size of a finished rose.

4 With wire cutters, cut a 3-to-4-in/ 7.5-to-10-cm length of grapevine wire. Use a dab of hot glue to attach it to the bottom of the rosebud.

5 Continue adding petals to the flower until you reach the finished size of the rose. Use the last petals to hide the hot glue on the bottom of the rose and to wrap around the top of the grapevine wire.

6 Repeat Steps 2–5 to make a second rose.

7 Trace and cut out 5 leaves from the green felt. Glue the two roses together on one side, holding them in place until the glue is dry. Then glue the leaves to the back of the roses, starting on one side and overlapping them slightly.

8 Wrap the grapevine stems with twine and tie together with a bow. Then with the faux pearl–head pin, pin in place just like a live flower boutonniere.

VARIATIONS

* Make a cluster of mini roses to mimic the look of a spray of roses.

* Use a single rose to simplify the project.

* Make the roses slightly smaller and use as corsages for the mother of the bride and the mother of the groom.

AILEEN LEIUTEN

BROOKLYN, NEW YORK

"I'm a Waldorf alumna and have always been around wool felt and natural materials. But it was only when my daughter started going to a Waldorf school about five years ago that I took workshops at the school," says Aileen. "I started creating with wool felt right away." Aileen finds inspiration in nature, books, and works of art. Her love for felt comes down to the material itself: "The soft, natural material keeps everything gentle and consistent in style." With an MFA in experimental animation, Aileen says, "Paying attention to detail and truly looking at everything around me has impacted all my work." In addition to her work with felt, Aileen writes and illustrates children's books (as does her husband), makes sculpture, and leads weekly craft workshops. "I need to create to be happy," she says. "I do have to switch it up to stay engaged, so I often try new mediums and make things I have never made before." The ability to take risks and to play comes across in much of her work, including the whimsical projects shown here.

"[Felt] is good for the environment, it's healthy for children to play with, and it always looks great. I enjoy working with other materials too, but I seem to gravitate back to wool felt."

FIND AILEEN
Aleijten.com   Feltforest.etsy.com

A more sophisticated version of a craft item you may have made as a child, this felt ornament will remind you how a simple exercise in creativity can lift your spirits. Make one, or many, depending on your own heart's desire.

MATERIALS

One 9-by-12-in/23-by-30.5-cm sheet of wool felt (such as plant-dyed wool felt from wierdollsandcrafts.com), in red or a color of your choosing

Cotton embroidery thread

One 3-to-6-in/7.5-to-15-cm piece of $\frac{1}{4}$-in/6-mm-wide ribbon

Cotton balls or wool roving

TOOLS

1 sheet of paper

Pinking shears or scissors

Embroidery needle

1. Make a heart template by folding the piece of paper in half and cutting out half of a heart shape in any size you like; the middle of the heart is on the fold of the paper (just like you used to do in grade school). This will be your heart template. Keep in mind that 2 of these heart templates will need to fit on your sheet of felt.

2. Using your template, cut out 2 hearts from the felt with pinking shears or scissors.

3. Cut an arm's length of embroidery thread, take 1 or 2 strands from the length of embroidery thread, and thread your needle. Tie a knot at the end of the long side of thread.

4. The size of the felt heart will determine the length of ribbon you will need to create a hanging loop for your heart. The heart pictured (see photo, page 120) measures 2½ in/6 cm wide and used a 3-in/7.5-cm piece of ribbon. If your heart measures larger than that, you may need a longer piece of ribbon. Fold the ribbon piece in half and stitch the bottom of both ribbon ends together. Sew the bottom of the ribbon loop to the inside of 1 of the hearts, just below the V in the heart. Take care not to go all the way through the felt so your stitches remain hidden. Don't cut the thread.

5. Line up the other felt heart over the one used in Step 4 and sew through it once so that the needle is on the outside of the second heart. Make sure both felt hearts are lined up and sew them together with a running stitch ¼ in/6 mm from the cut heart edge.

6. When you are a little over halfway around the heart, stuff the heart with cotton balls or wool roving. When you have given the heart a nice shape but you can still close the edges, hold the hearts together and finish stitching around.

7. Make a double knot in your thread, sew through to the opposite side once, and cut your thread to finish.

VARIATIONS

* Make the ribbon loop longer and use to decorate interior doorknobs.

* Change up the colors and use the hearts in mobiles, garlands, or decorative clusters.

* Use the hearts to top holiday packages, and add embellishments that you desire.

Woodland in spirit and whimsical in nature, this decorative mushroom is an exercise in playfulness. Make one, or a handful, and use them to brighten up nooks around your house.

MATERIALS

One 6-by-4-in/15-by-10-cm piece of wool felt, in white

One 3-by-3-in/7.5-by-7.5-cm piece of wool felt, in red (such as plant-dyed wool felt from wierdollsandcrafts.com)

2 skeins cotton embroidery thread, in white and red

Cotton balls (optional)

White wool roving

TOOLS

Mushroom Template

Disappearing fabric marker

Scissors

Embroidery needle

Felting needle

1 Using the Magic Mushroom Template, trace and cut 1 mushroom stem with the rectangle shape and 1 mushroom top with the circle out of white felt. Then cut a second mushroom top out of red felt.

2 Cut off about an arm's length of white embroidery thread and thread your embroidery needle with 2 or 3 strands. Tie a knot at the end of the long side of thread.

3 On the short straight side of the mushroom stem piece, place 2 small backstitches toward one of the corners, which will anchor your thread and hide the knot. Starting at the straight short side, with the needle and thread pulled out of the way, roll the mushroom stem piece tightly into a log shape. Holding the rolled stem tightly, push the needle and thread through all the layers of the stem from the center to the outside edge of your felt. You will want the needle to exit the felt, catching the outside edge, about 1/8 in/3 mm from the edge.

4 Sew the outside overlapped edge of the felt securely to the stem using a whipstitch. Make a knot in your thread after you reach the top of the log. Do not cut the thread.

5 Cut a tiny hole in the center of the white mushroom top. Pull the needle and thread through the hole in the mushroom top. Center the mushroom top over the top of the mushroom stem and sew through the center of the stem so your needle comes out right under the edge of the mushroom top. With a whipstitch, sew the bottom of the mushroom top to the mushroom stem. Pull the needle through to the top of the mushroom top, then knot and cut the thread.

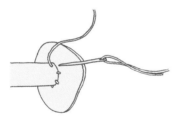

6 Cut off about an arm's length of red embroidery thread and thread your embroidery needle. Tie a knot at the end of the long side of thread. Sew through the edge of the red mushroom top to fasten your thread, then place the red mushroom top on top of the white mushroom top, with the knot side down. Align all edges and sew the red and white mushroom tops together with a running stitch, about 1/8 in/3 mm from the edge.

7 Once you have the mushroom tops sewn a bit over half together, stuff with either cotton balls or wool roving until they have a slightly rounded shape but you can still close the edges. Keep in mind that the stuffing will shrink slightly over time, so you can overstuff your mushroom slightly. Finish sewing around the edge, then knot off at the end. Pull the thread between both mushroom tops and out the top and cut to hide the thread.

8 With the wool roving, form little balls (approximately 1/8-to-1/4-in/3-to-6-mm diameter in size) by rolling small pieces between your thumb and index finger. Place 1 of the wool balls on the red top of the mushroom and pierce it over and over with the felting needle until it is attached; repeat to make more white dots on the mushroom top until you like the look.

VARIATIONS

* Sew a ribbon loop onto the top of the mushroom to turn it into an ornament.

* Make a few mushrooms with different colored tops to create a little collection.

* Use a mushroom as a pincushion to store an assortment of pins and needles.

WHERE TO SOURCE SUPPLIES

Some of the best felt can be found online, where it's sold by real folks who care about the quality. Here are some of my favorite sources.

FELT ON THE FLY

Feltonthefly.etsy.com

The selection of pure wool felt includes 96 colors, a variety of thickness and sheet sizes, and handy color charts so you know exactly what you're ordering.

FILZ FELT

Filzfelt.com

Your source for German-milled, 100-percent wool felt in 54 Pantone colors and 5 thickness options. Larger yardage is available if you prefer to purchase in bulk.

GIANT DWARF

Giantdwarf.etsy.com

Cut-to-order Fancy Felt is 70-percent wool and 30-percent viscose, making it extremely durable and easy to craft with.

LUPIN HANDMADE

Lupinhandmade.com

Laura Howard's shop is a fantastic source for felt sheets and packets of felt squares. She stocks colors that can be hard to find elsewhere.

MATERIAL EVIDENCE

Materialevidenceshop.etsy.com

100-percent wool felt in every colorway imaginable, including a lovely selection of heathered wool.

PURL SOHO

Purlsoho.com

Purl Soho carries felt from multiple vendors, including 100-percent Wollfilz wool felt, which is highly regarded. The shop's felt bundles easily compel you to develop a weakness for the material.

Whether you visit in person or online, independent craft shops always offer something unexpected and inspiring, which is most often tied to the fact that the super passionate shop owners are stocking the shelves. Here are some wonderful craft shops.

BROOKLYN GENERAL STORE

Brooklyngeneral.com
128 Union Street
Brooklyn, NY 11231

Catherine Clark and Katie Metzger created Brooklyn General to sell yarn, fabric, notions, and dry goods to city folk.

FOUND

Foundgallery.com
407 North Fifth Avenue
Ann Arbor, MI 48104

Vintage treasures, new handmade works, and notions galore fill this curiosity shop. Visits are as good for collecting inspiration as they are for stocking up.

PURL SOHO

Purlsoho.com
459 Broome Street
New York, NY 10013

In addition to a solid assortment of felt offerings, the shop (online or in person) stocks a wonderful assortment of yarn, notions, and books galore. You might want to pick up some fabric while you're there; their selection is hard to beat.

SEW L.A.

Sew-la.com
1637 ½ Silver Lake Boulevard
Los Angeles, CA 90026

Visit for sewing classes and tutorials, as well as fabric and notions.

SPACECRAFT

Spacecraftbrooklyn.com
355 Bedford Avenue
Brooklyn, NY 11211

Part workshop space, part craft store, Spacecraft is a community-minded creative space. They have classes, space for you to throw a party, or even a work space so you can finish your own project.

URBAN ARTS AND CRAFTS

Urbanartsandcrafts.com
4165 North Mulberry Drive
Kansas City, MO 64116

This store is a crafter's dream come true. With beads, yarn, paper, ribbon, buttons, fabric, and anything in between that you might need, this shop has it all.

URBAN FAUNA STUDIO

Urbanfaunastudio.com

UFS sells independent and sustainable yarn, notions, and craft supplies. They host workshops and rent studio space and equipment (like spinning wheels) by the hour.

WILD FIBRE

Wildfibreyarns.com
6 East Liberty Street
Savannah, GA 31401

This is a fiber arts and yarn shop where students and grads of the Savannah College of Art and Design (SCAD) go to stock up.

Here are the go-to spots for scissors, beads, ribbons, embroidery thread, buttons, and so much more.

BUTTON & CRAFT

Coatsandclark.com

This is thick and sturdy sewing thread for securing embellishments (and hand-stitching).

DMC

Dmc-usa.com

DMC threads are widely available and useful for embellishing and finishing. The site also features instructional videos and tutorials for everything from crochet to cross-stitch.

FIRE MOUNTAIN GEMS AND BEADS

Firemountaingems.com

A wealth of supplies includes seed and bugle beads, crystals, and jewelry supplies, including clasps, hooks, and earring and pin bases.

GINGHER

Gingher.com

Gingher is one of the most trusted companies for sewing scissors and notions, like seam rippers, rotary cutters, and rulers. Gingher products are extremely well made and will last for years if used as intended.

M&J TRIMMING

Mjtrim.com
1008 Sixth Avenue
New York, NY 10018

Buttons, buckles, handles, appliqués, and cords make this an excellent place to stock up on design and crafting accessories.

TINSEL TRADING COMPANY

Tinseltrading.com
1 West 37th Street
New York, NY 10018

Manhattan's finest trimmings shop—which started in the 1930s as an importer of metal thread—features ribbon, embellishments, paper, tassels, buttons, and floral delights.

WEEKS DYE WORKS

Weeksdyeworks.com

Weeks carries hand-overdyed embroidery floss in a gorgeous spectrum of colors. They also offer hand-dyed wool fabric, sewing thread, and pearl cotton.

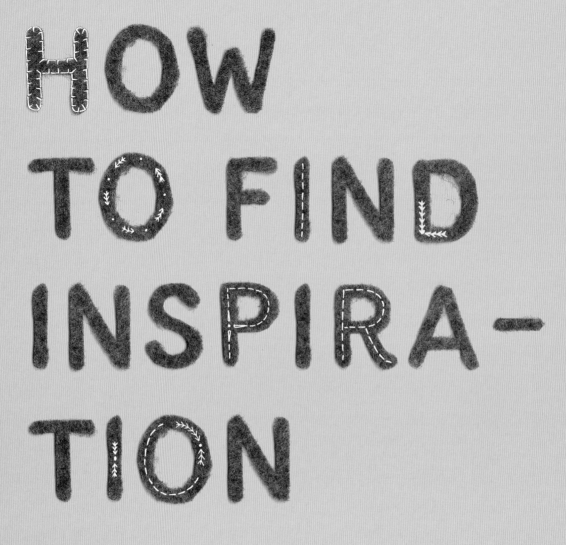

HOW TO FIND INSPIRA- TION

Seeing what other creative people are making can be inspirational and motivational. Here are some of the best places to visit to stir your creative juices.

ANGRYCHICKEN.TYPEPAD.COM
Crafter and author Amy Karol shares her unique take on living a crafty life—complete with projects and recipes.

BLOG.BETZWHITE.COM
An author, designer, and green crafter, Betz is always sharing delightful ideas. Follow for news about her latest projects.

BLOG.LENACORWIN.COM
Lena Corwin's observations and inspirations cover a wide range of design, fabric, pattern, and craft eye candy.

BUGSANDFISHES
.BLOGSPOT.COM
Laura Howard (see page 100) shares creative projects, tutorials, and inspiration—much of which revolves around felt.

DIGSANDBEAN
.BLOGSPOT.COM
Craft book author and blogger Amanda Carestio blogs about her latest projects and her crafty life.

FRESHLYCHOPPED
.BLOGSPOT.COM
Artist, designer, and all-around creative lady Leah Duncan shares the behind-the-scenes of her work. The pictures alone will inspire you to make something.

GARMENTHOUSE
.BLOGSPOT.COM
Elly of Garment House is always making impressive knits and sewn pieces. Her style is unique and intriguing and offers a nice dose of creative perspective.

MAKEGROWGATHER.COM
Kelly Wilkinson, author of *Weekend Handmade*, shares DIY projects that range from crafts to home, food, and gardening.

MAKESOMETHING.CA
Karyn Valino's online home is a wealth of crafty eye candy.

OHHAPPYDAY.COM
Jordan Ferney is a West Coast party planner and letterpress printer who has a knack for all things DIY. Be sure to check out her in-depth (and well-designed) tutorials.

PINTEREST.COM
If you're not on Pinterest yet, it's time to get an account. It's the perfect place to keep track of projects, resources, and inspiration as you travel the Web, mood board style.

**ROSYLITTLETHINGS
.TYPEPAD.COM**
Where stitchery maven Alicia Paulsen
blogs about life and creations. Follow
to stay in the know about her pattern
releases.

SOULEMAMA.TYPEPAD.COM
Amanda Blake Soule shares all
about her creative family life and
her handmade home. Her day-to-day
is an inspiring look at how to infuse
creativity into each moment.

**THECRAFTSDEPT
.MARTHASTEWART.COM**
The very talented folks of Martha
Stewart's crafts department share
daily inspiration, tools, and projects.

THEPURLBEE.COM
The online channel of Purl Soho,
filled with projects and tutorials.

WHIPUP.NET
A crafty forum to share projects with
fellow creatives, from Australia-based
Kathreen Ricketson.

*Fa la la la Felt: 45 Handmade
Holiday Decorations*
by Amanda Carestio
Sweet projects to make the best use
of your felt stash for the holidays.

*Kata Golda's Hand-Stitched Felt:
25 Whimsical Sewing Projects*
by Kata Golda
Chock full of toys and home accessories
that are sweet and stylish—and just a
tiny bit imperfect.

*Sewing Green: 25 Projects Made
with Repurposed & Organic
Materials*
by Betz White
Sustainably minded projects will
remind you that turning trash into
treasure (and sweaters into wool felt)
is way fun.

*Super-Cute Felt: 35 Step-by-Step
Projects to Make and Give*
by Laura Howard
Sweet, feminine, and happiness-
inducing, this is one felt book that
will bring a little levity to your craft
book shelf.

*Warm Fuzzies: 30 Sweet
Felted Projects*
by Betz White
Learn the ins and outs of recycled
felting with this sweet collection
of creations.

Here are a few tools to help you take your stitching and embroidery to the next level.

Alabama Stitch Book
by Natalie Chanin

This lovely book includes projects that celebrate and teach the history of hand-stitchery. The emphasis on decorative stitches makes this a must-read.

Elegant Stitches
by Judith Baker Montano

This book is essential for your craft library—it has every embroidery technique a girl could ever want.

Martha Stewart's Encyclopedia of Sewing and Fabric Crafts

This book contains detailed illustrations and definitions of stitching techniques that you may find helpful.

DMC.COM

On this website, under the "education" tab, watch videos on surface embroidery, how to get started with an embroidery needle, and basic embroidery stitches.

MARTHASTEWART.COM/ HOW-TO/EMBROIDERY

This web page offers a basic guide to getting started on all things related to embroidery, from the crafts department at Martha Stewart.

Index

Transforming a basic material like felt into countless creative and inspiring projects takes talent. Thank you to Yoko, Stephanie, Faith, Lindy, Jill, Kasia, Jen, Sandie, Jeanie, Laura, Nicole, and Aileen for allowing me the opportunity to share your work. Gratitude to Laura Lee Mattingly, Stefanie Von Borstel, Julia Rothman, Adam Holt, and Allison Weiner for bringing the projects to life within these pages.

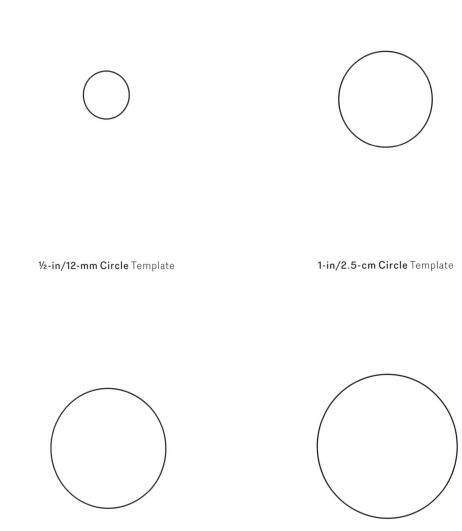

½-in/12-mm **Circle** Template

1-in/2.5-cm **Circle** Template

1¼-in/3.25-cm **Circle** Template

1½-in/4-cm **Circle** Template

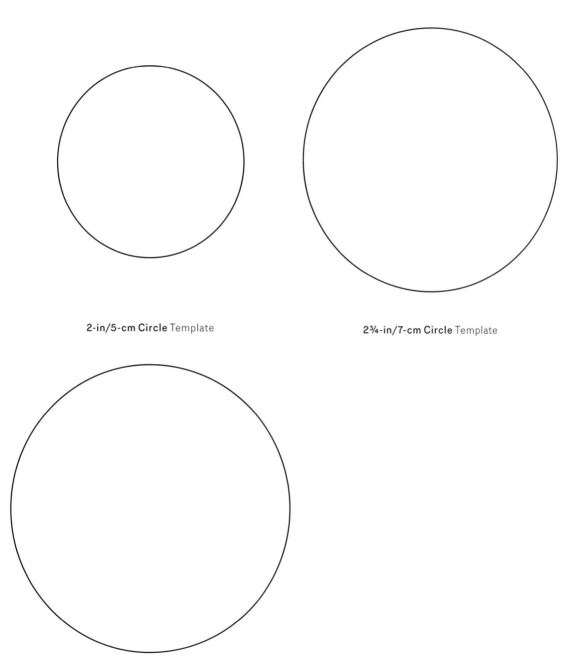

2-in/5-cm Circle Template

2¾-in/7-cm Circle Template

3-in/7.5-cm Circle Template

C H E E R S

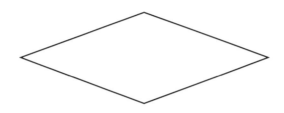

Cupcake Toppers Template
(C-H-E-E-R-S letters and diamond)

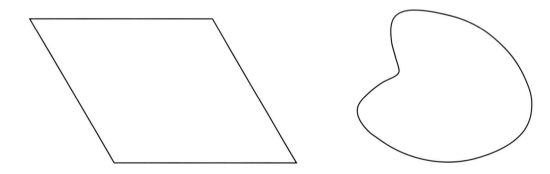

Graphic Table Runner Template

Carnation Corsage Template

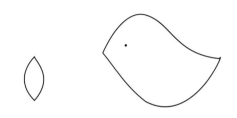

Birdie Bag Template — Enlarge by 125% (leaf, bird, and rectangle)

Helen Fascinator Pattern

Sharon Headband Pattern — Enlarge by 143%

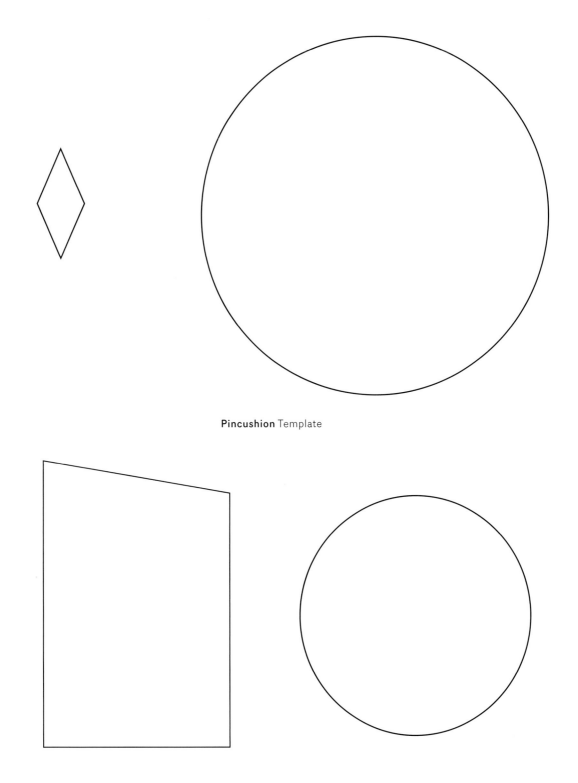

Pincushion Template

Magic Mushroom Template (stem and top)

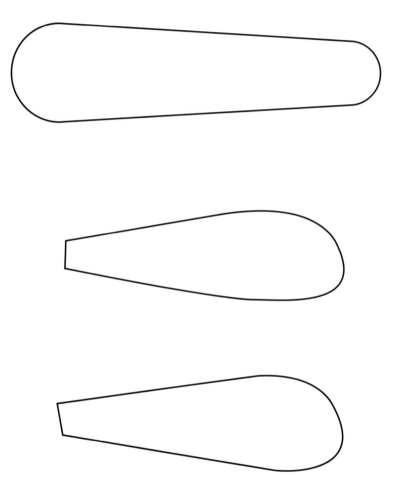

Dragonfly Pennant Template (body, wings, and dragonfly)

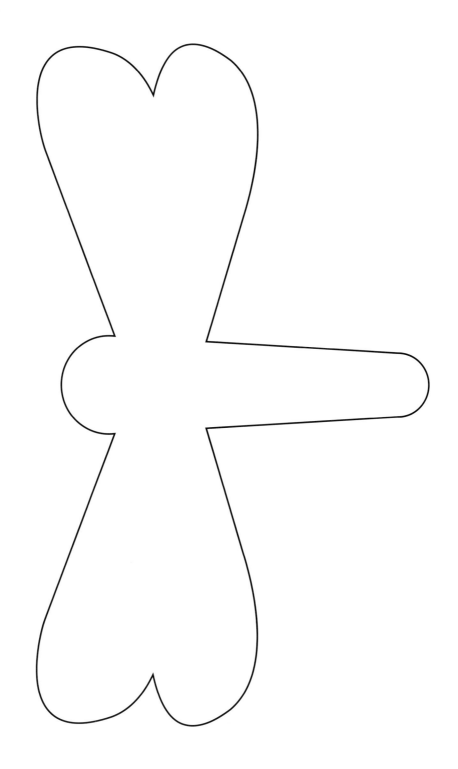